C000009968

'SMARVELI
More Musical M........

PREVIOUSLY PUBLISHED
BY THE AUTHOR

S'Wonderful

'Smarvellous

More Musical Memories

TONY IRELAND

JOHN NICKALLS PUBLICATIONS

First published 2003
© Tony Ireland 2003

*All rights reserved. No part of this publication
may be reproduced, in any form or by any means,
without the prior consent of the author.*

ISBN 1 904136 12 5

Front cover: Tony Ireland in concert,
by Charles Nicholas.

Back cover: Tony and Miriam, taken on board
the *SS Canberra,* 1995

Published by John Nickalls Publications,
Oak Farm Bungalow, Sawyers Lane, Suton,
Wymondham, Norfolk NR18 9SH

Designed by Ashley Gray and Printed by Geo R Reeve Ltd,
9–11 Town Green, Wymondham, Norfolk NR18 0BD

Contents

Foreword

AS Tony says in his book, Musicians seldom meet – particularly Piano Players, they are always 'on duty' working all day and doing 'Gigs' at night. Consequently during my 30 years as Musical Director at Anglia Television I had, of course, heard of Tony Ireland, his various bands, and the work he undertook acting as accompanist (usually unpaid) to many local artistes, choirs and societies.

It seemed to be a case of 'Need a good pianist?' send for Ireland he can play anything. But we had never met until that Sunday some seven or eight years ago when Shirley and I took Sunday lunch at The Oaklands Hotel. Seated at the piano was a very miserable-looking chap playing all the 'nice tunes' on a most appalling instrument. It was out of tune with itself, some keys didn't work and it made it seem like he was playing all the right notes but not necessarily in the right order – just like Eric Morecambe. I approached this poor chap and told him in no uncertain terms what to do with the instrument. It was of course Tony and we became instant friends and the rest, as they say, is history.

Tony has a prodigious memory. I believe that nearly everybody he has played for, or worked with, is mentioned in this book or the previous instalment. You will know all the tunes and most of the shows and locations he mentions.

We remain very close friends and as with most musicians, like taking the mickey out of each other. I still take great delight in marching into The Oaklands on a Sunday and demanding (in a loud voice): "The third movement of Harrison Birtwhistles 2nd Symphony," or failing that, "can't you play nothing by The Stoones then?"

Read and enjoy.

Peter Fenn

Introduction

THIS book, the sequel to *S'Wonderful*, was written in response to the many genuine requests I have had from people who had read the first. Besides, *S'Wonderful* ended in 1989 with my retirement from the teaching profession and at the end of the last chapter I declared that another book would have to follow, since so much had happened to me since then.

In it, I wandered down the many wonderful musical roads that life has led me, for music has been my guide over the years, and it is something for which I am so grateful.

'Smarvellous is the second line of the Gershwin song for which I make no apologies but rather use it in honour of the man who leads my list of American composers who, together with brother Ira, gave the world such astounding music and song.

My book is dedicated to all those wonderful musicians, particularly of course, pianists, some of whom I have known personally, some I have only heard and others I have never seen, who each in their own way have played their part in shaping my musical life.

I would also like to thank the following people for their help in compiling this book: my wife Miriam for all the computer work, Wendy and Oz Topliff, Paul Donley, Ian Harrison, Peter Fenn, John Nickalls, David Valentine, Derek James and Ashley Gray.

Tony Ireland
May 2003

CHAPTER ONE

Nice Work
If You Can Get It

WHEN retirement dawned for me late in July 1989 I wondered how I would feel. To some people, retirement was a word to strike terror: I knew many who dreaded it, including those in the teaching profession who hadn't the faintest idea what they might do with their lives. So many of those teachers having no hobby or pastime returned to the classroom, either on a part-time or permanent basis. Even had I wanted to do this, my premature retirement on health grounds precluded my taking classroom work. There was little doubt that I presented a very sickly countenance and, indeed, that photograph in the local paper prior to my departure from Thorpe Hamlet gave the appearance of a strong candidate for a walk-on part in *Dance Macabre*. The bathroom mirror didn't reveal any difference and I gazed at a cadaverous-looking reflection which certainly suggested I need seek physical and mental help.

The retirement photograph seemed to trigger off dozens of telephone enquiries for my musical services and, indeed, the very next day there came a call from a lady who wondered if I might be interested in becoming conductor of her choir, something I politely declined since this was not my forté and I was in any case already pianist to the Taverham Singers.

My pedal leg was giving me a great deal of pain, the result of a less than perfect operation in 1975 when yards of vein had been pulled from me, some very third-rate embroidery stitching done, and after care that would have made Florence Nightingale burst a blood vessel. Despite there being an upright piano in that ward at Wayland, to which I was drawn (as I am to most), I was unable to let the patients have the benefit of my playing, seeing that my right leg was swathed in several hundred feet of bandage and was at least the size of a tree trunk. So it was that, instead of being restored to full working and walking order, I was to endure considerable pain for a long time to come, which intensified during Jane's illness and demise.

Despite the aggravation of a nagging leg pain I decided that music would be my main interest in retirement, and that I would, as they say, listen to any offers which came my way. These came in three varieties: paid, 'we haven't an awful lot of money' and what musicians term 'God Bless You' jobs. There were plenty in the offing of categories two and three, which would discount any idea of on retirement doing absolutely nothing, but at the same time rule out any thoughts of a vast income. I suppose doing nothing would be mooching round the city (perish the thought), or sitting in a local park watching the world go by, which wouldn't have its appeal, particularly in driving rain and a gale force eight! Remember Fred Astaire and Ginger Rogers, 'Isn't It A Lovely Day'? Anyway, neither of those ideas appealed to me and I listened to any offers coming my way.

At the same time, I received bits of advice and suggestions from friends – mainly married friends, on relieving my leg discomfort. Paul Donley, conductor of the Taverham Singers, for whom I was pianist, had a nagging thumb pain for which he was receiving treatment from James Scott-Robinson, a rugby-loving jazz guitarist who made a living sticking needles into people. Since Paul seemed to have benefitted from James' needles I decided to give it a try and popped along to his St Giles Street rooms where I was greeted in the most friendly way by James – jovial, bearded and armed to the teeth with needles!

For many a session of acupuncture (the technical term) I lay on a table, head propped on a pillow, and was impregnated with needles in most parts of my anatomy, large ones in the more expansive areas, and little ones in ear lobes and other small corners. James, seemingly knowing what he was doing, tended to find it amusing and recounted how he had on one occasion gone to answer the telephone and left a patient to 'over-cook' with the needles left sticking in him.

I reminded James of the Norfolk codger who decided he didn't believe in all them there injections, filling people full o' holes, enough to make them die o' draughts. I had thought that the most important thing for open discussion would be my leg, but uppermost in conversation were the merits of jazz guitarists like D'Jango Reinhardt and Eddie Lang, which I supposed was all part of James' therapy. Many a session I spent on James' table with more needles than a porcupine, and many an in-depth discussion about jazz.

Did the session help? To a degree, but the pain remained.

Tony Cleary, bass-playing architect, told me that his mother-in-law, suffering with something I-know-not-what, had consulted a certain Indian guru down in Suffolk who seemed to be doing her some good. Tony suggested I give this gentleman a look with a view to helping my affliction, which took me down to a sleepy village just over the border to find Dr Singh housed in a large county mansion in spacious grounds. I don't remember that his name was actually Singh, but many Indians are, and it does sound musical! The good doctor, who might have hailed from Hyderabad or Handsworth (I know not), spoke just like Peter Sellers, and I nearly burst into "Oh Doctor I'm in trouble", with he responding, "Goodness gracious me!", but I desisted. As it was, from his row of gleaming white teeth he uttered his first mystic words: "That will be £50 for the first consultation. Cash or cheque?"

After he had safely pocketed my fee, Dr Singh then asked me lots of questions, some of which seemed quite irrelevant, and then wrote on a scrap of paper these directions, 'For one week eat only 16 large oranges a day and drink only hot water'. He did suggest that the consumption of that quantity of oranges each day could be made easier by grilling them in halves – and please come back next week with your cheque book!

There was more than a mild look of surprise on the face of the girl at the supermarket check-out when I produced two baskets of 96 Seville oranges, which must have been matched by mirth when she announced the total cost.

I ventured to telephone Tony's mother-in-law since I was somewhat concerned that an intake of so many oranges would have considerable consequences from an alimentary point of view. It was a question which I tried to convey as delicately as I could, "I am supposed to eat sixteen oranges a day – did they give cause for you to remain near a bathroom?"

"Oh I had nothing like that. I have to eat twelve pounds of grapes per day."

"Oh."

"And no – I've had no problems such as you describe."

So, it was a case of wait and see, with my religiously grilling four oranges for breakfast, four for lunch, four for tea and – yes – four more for supper, washed down with a delicious cup of hot Chateau Yare!

My daughter Elisabeth received it all with a mixture of doubt and amusement, with some added sympathy, whilst I wondered when hunger would manifest itself. At that time I was escorting Catherine Soame-Hook to various functions, but I could hardly have taken her to a restaurant to have a four-course dinner with wine while I sat opposite with grilled oranges and a glass of hot water. I think Catherine was more horrified than amused.

The following Saturday, with hunger pangs just starting, I again tripped off to Suffolk and Dr Singh, to his waiting room along with other mugs (sorry – patients) and, after duly handing over £35, received a familiar handwritten note which read, 'Eat ten pounds of raw vegetables a day. Continue hot water'.

Now knowing the routine I purchased about three tons of Peter Rabbit food and spent the week forcing the salad down, together with the delights of a glass of Eau Chaud. By the time I was to return for further oriental treatment I had begun to take on the wan appearance which gave cause for comment, particularly from among members of the Taverham Singers who possibly were afraid I might slip down the grating in Drayton Methodist church, their practice home.

Dr Singh, presumably well-pleased with my progress (if one could call it such), gave me great hope when, after ensuring receipt of my next cheque, allowed me to eat raw fish and imbibe hot tea with no milk. You can imagine my gratitude at this as I plundered the delicatessen at the supermarket for the sort of things normally reserved for sea-lions or penguins. When, at the next consultation, Dr Singh had me lying naked on a table in order to strike needles in me where it took his fancy, I decided to call it a day. Being prepared for the call from his secretary to arrange the next appointment, I assumed the guise of Mr Ireland's 'man' who informed her that his master had emigrated!

What, you may ask, did Dr Singh do for me? Well, he made me lose pounds, both avoir-dupois and sterling, and reduced me to a mere wraith which gave cause for concern to many, again the ladies of the choir. He had successfully given me an abhorrence of oranges, raw vegetables, and raw fish. It occurred to me that he might also have owned an orange grove, a vineyard, and a fish farm. Certainly the expense made me realise I had to 'pick myself up, dust myself off, and start all over again', to quote Jerome Kern's song.

One day in the supermarket I met an ex-colleague who, like me, had been a head of music in a Norwich school. I asked him how he was enjoying his retirement, to which he pulled a face, obviously indicating he was not.

"Well", I said, "remember – musicians never retire – they just go from bar to bar." He, being a most unusual musician, having no sense of humour at all, declared he never touched alcohol and that my quote could not apply to him!

Of course, I could have said the other one: musicians never retire – they just de-compose, but I thought better of it and, in all seriousness, decided that it was something I certainly wouldn't do: on the contrary, I needed to think about the music in my life. Did it have charm? Would it soothe the savage breast – or at least my leg? Most of all, could it be the food of love? In which case I yearned for excess of it.

All this would yet be revealed.

CHAPTER TWO

At the Jazz Band Ball

YARE Valley Jazz, the brain-child of Paul Donley, was a somewhat haphazard phenomenon called together rather like making up a four for bridge.

It happened to be four which usually consisted of Paul on clarinet, Tony Cleary on 'steam' bass, Don Brewer on drums, and me on piano. Other musicians occasionally 'depped' like Mike Harris and Gill Alexander (bass), and Rex Cooper or David Donley (Paul's son) on drums. With such a line-up the sound was more of the swing variety, hinting of Benny Goodman or Artie Shaw, with not a written crotchet among us, everything being 'head arranged' as they say in the music business. I never remember a practice or rehearsal but a mere piece of paper on which Paul had listed jazz numbers quick and slow to select from for the gig, which I suppose was flattering to all that he had the confidence we would all play the same number at the same time with the chords harmonizing between us. Mind you, when any jazz men get together they generally blend from the first bar to the last, where the cry is: "Make mine a double!"

Paul, as leader on the clarinet, flung himself into it with vigorous enthusiasm with chorus after chorus, changing his complexion from deep pink to dark purple, which at times seemed to worry the ladies of the Taverham Singers during the jazz interludes.

Like many blowers of the 'licorice stick' Paul had his problems with either temperamental reeds or leaks in the plumbing. With the former he would try out a selection of reeds, casting aside those that offended and trying to make good those he found passable. Indeed, I remember Benny Goodman saying, in a box of loose reeds he might only find a couple to keep, while a musician friend, Joe McKenna (who taught me clarinet), said he had once seen the great English clarinet player, Carl Barriteau take a full box of reeds and smash the lot. Clearly it wasn't just the reeds that were temperamental.

With the leaks, Paul would carry a supply of elastic bands, sellotape, and blu-tack, no doubt familiar accessories to those of you who play the clarinet. Paul also played with the South Norfolk Wind Band for whom he worked as coach and deputy conductor, and it was from them he would borrow an ancient bass clarinet which certainly needed the equivalent of a cylinder head gasket and, in all probability, a complete re-bore.

When he reverted to a solo or two during performance it (or he) would give off distinctly odd sounds which caused the listening dance couples to wear surprised looks, and for Paul to peer into the bell as if half expecting a foreign body to emerge. I have to say I suspect that many of the sounds which emanated from that bass clarinet, whilst fairly effective, were not entirely intentional! After each solo, Paul would beam a grin from ear to ear and chuckle gleefully which, to me, indicated he was either satisfied or highly amused by what had gone into the atmosphere.

The 'library' was split into two lists – quicks and slows, such as 'I Got Rhythm' and 'Georgia' with nothing in 3/4, Paul relying on me producing a waltz should anyone have the temerity to ask for one. I have heard jazz musicians display complete ignorance when a waltz is mentioned, although Jerome Kern actually wrote a clever piece called 'Waltz in Swing Time'.

Of course, choruses went on interminably, making you wonder when, or if, the number would ever finish (it's like that with jazz), and only by watching Paul's eyes or finger, or both, could you know the last bars were due. Occasionally, someone would mis-read his semaphore and carry on regardless thus breaking the belief that everyone would finish together.

Tony Cleary, a handsome South African-born architect, was the bass-player, married to Adrienne, commonly called Ren, and at the time living in a very large listed house in Ashwellthorpe. For a very long time I thought his wife's name was 'Wren' due to her bird-like way!

Tony played the straight music with the Wymondham Phil but enjoyed making up the foursome with Yare Valley Jazz, playing in his own inimitable way, which was often with eyes tightly closed for most of a number. He would appear to be totally transported to ethereal places, or 'gone man' in jazz parlance, taking innumerable choruses which became progressively frenetic or, again, in jazz terms, 'way out' man.

Tony believed in playing bass in a sitting position, unlike many who preferred to stand. Mind you, I have seen, bass players in the supine position but they were definitely not playing at the time! Tony Cleary seated himself on an old tractor seat, though I should point out here that the rest of the tractor had been removed, and that the perforated-metal seat was welded to a stand.

His sense of humour was ever-present in all we did and is best described as droll, some of his tales having us all in fits.

Don Brewer, on the drums, was, to put it mildly, a bit man of 'XXXL' variety with a huge laugh to match. He had worked for many years in the film industry – no, not as a movie star but in the technical world of the silver screen. Living at Sparham he and his wife Dee ran a fleet of coaches, occupying his spare time playing percussion for many bands in the Norfolk area.

When 'man mountain' Don arrived for a gig you heard him afar off since he came armed with a massive amount of kit which probably contained several tons of scaffolding, with its owner audibly groaning and wheezing under its weight. With my first introduction to him I went to help carry a case and promptly staggered.

Of course, with such a huge kit Don had to have something big in transport to carry him and it, which was why he arrived in a very large campervan that contained everything – yes, including the kitchen sink!

Don also sang (or vocalized as the expression is) which gave light relief to the constant band sound, and he did have a pleasing way of putting over a jazzy number, particularly 'Sweet Lorraine', it being the name of his daughter and he being a great fan of Nat King Cole.

Sadly, Dee died of cancer after a long drawn-out illness, and I was able to offer Don what little help I could from my own personal experiences. He quit the coach business but, to his credit, kept up the band work which was so vital to keep his mind occupied and easing the grief.

Who's the fourth hand? Well, two hands really – mine. I played piano, with the usual assortment of mostly clapped-out horrors, until Paul decided to buy a keyboard which made life easier and also gave an alternative sound at the press of a button – that of vibes. It meant that we could sound exactly like Benny Goodman and Lionel Hampton: well, not exactly, but passably good.

So what of the gigs with Yare Valley Jazz?

Well, to put it mildly, most were rather unusual. During the day Paul worked as a commercial artist in the advertising business, through which he got to know a great number of people, some of whom called on his services as a musician. There were a couple of new car promotions, for example, the first of which was down at Bury St Edmunds playing in a show room with some brand new Ford (or was it Vauxhall?) cars with jolly accessories like champagne and delicious vol-au-vents, but alas no free samples!

There was a similar one in Norwich, at Lancasters, where a new Porsche was being displayed at a knock down price of £85,000, and although we all took a turn sitting in it, were not allowed to take a sample away. There was jazz galore under a blazing sun, drinks and food in plenty, and we actually got paid too, though I do recall one of us asking for a new model in lieu of payment. However, Lancasters didn't find that idea acceptable.

Then there was jazz at a Christmas trade fair for people in business, held at an enormous warehouse on a Norwich industrial estate. It was heaving with every kind of Christmas decoration you could imagine, from Christmas trees which sang 'Jingle Bells' to Father Christmases that wobbled their stomachs as they uttered the magic words: "Ho, Ho, Ho" to the accompaniment of 'Rudolf the Red-Nosed Reindeer'. I love the story behind 'Rudolf'. Apparently, Johnny Marks, the American song writer, was down on his uppers as he gazed into a toy shop window one Christmas. There, amongst all the toys, was a small reindeer with a red nose called Rudolf (the deer, not the nose) and the song came into his mind, with the rest, as they say, becoming part of history. I expect Johnny Marks made a fortune: if he did, good luck to him. If he didn't, then he must have picked the wrong publishers!

The warehouse in question was not only huge, it was perishing cold, despite a couple of heaters placed near where we were to play. I sat near one and gradually thawed, enabling me to play with most of my fingers and walk as far as the table which proffered wines and soft drinks but (you're ahead of me!), not at the same time.

Rolls, sandwiches, cakes and other tit-bits appeared and, between playing sessions, we fortified ourselves to prevent keeling over from lack of food. Paul obviously knew the owner of the company who seemed well pleased with our efforts and wondered if we could stay until Easter. Well no, actually, come back then. Another successful one!

The second visit was there – much the same as the first – the Christmas paraphernalia being replaced with spring chickens and things, I think, and, as I remember, it was just as cold.

Frederick Norton, in his famous musical *Chu Chin Chow* has a song entitled 'Any Time's Kissing Time'. Could the 'kissing' be changed for 'jazz' I wondered? Well, not in most people's books, but the forward-thinking, somewhat eccentric, headmaster of New Buckenham School thought Jazz might be an appropriate accompaniment to breakfast! Breakfast?! Yes, a charity raising breakfast at his school with full English breakfast, and enjoyed to the sound of Yare Valley Jazz. So it was that Paul hoisted me from my slumbers on a bright sunny morning to shoot off down the B 1113 in time for a jazz breakfast at 7.30am, an hour probably not contemplated by most musicians.

Alongside serving tables laden with various cereals and fruit juices we set up with the alluring aroma of bacon and eggs and other lovely things cooking in the kitchen. I thought we should have swung with 'Big Butter and Egg Man' but perhaps Paul didn't know that and we kicked off with an up-tempo 'Sweet Georgia Brown'.

Throughout that jazz breakfast we all four salivated in anticipation, for our own breakfast was to follow – and what a feast it was. Young ladies with ladles served us with eggs, bacon, sausage, tomatoes, beans, mushrooms, and fried bread, a ton of cholesterol, together with jugs of fruit juice and pots of hot coffee. Of course, the whole event being a charity I think the breakfast was our just reward, by which I mean, just that and nothing else. We must have made an impression with the parents, staff and children since the headmaster booked us again.

The Head was all for innovation when it came to fund-raising with one idea being an art exhibition/sale, accompanied by none other than Yare Valley Jazz. I'm not sure I'd relish having a jazz band play as I viewed paintings, especially if I were contemplating a purchase, but apparently people did. That evening has to be remembered, not for its splendid paintings, not for the many colourful visitors, nor the supper on offer, (no? Really?) but for the bitter cold of the room where we played. All of us, by the end, were perishing cold, sans-heating, despite wearing our outdoor coats. It certainly added a realism to the painting of winter scenes, and I remember arriving home to make up a whiskey mac and two hot-water bottles.

I mentioned earlier about 'God Bless You' gigs, which to a musician means that no hint of any payment is made by the person booking the soloist or band, together with a kind of unspoken expectancy of no mention of the subject from the musician either. It is assumed that you are highly conversant with the fact that Mrs Smythe-Jenkinson's niece is running an orphanage single-handed in a remote part of Bessarabia, and that every penny is going there, including any fee that might otherwise have been discussed.

However, the other kind of 'God Bless You' gig is when you are employed to play for ministers of the cloth, and here Paul Donley managed not one bishop, but two!

The first was for a big charity garden party in the grounds of the Bishop's Palace in Norwich with Bishop Peter (Nott) in office. It was a boiling hot day to match the hot music of Yare Valley Jazz and it wasn't long before we discarded jackets. Of course, there were some folk there who at first clearly disapproved of the hideous din we made, although on hearing that the bishop was a keen follower of jazz music seemed to change their opinion. I seem to remember we did two sessions while in between sampled some delightful refreshments washed down with something rather lovely in a glass.

Mrs Nott, the bishop's wife, noting her husband's pleasure at the noises we were making, managed to corner Paul on his own to enlist the services of Yare Valley Jazz for his 60th birthday (the bishop's, not Paul's). It was to be a secret for a surprise dinner to be given in the palace. It actually turned out exactly as planned and even if Bishop Peter had half an idea of the event he didn't show it. Besides us there were several other famous people present, including some politicians. We had veteran drummer Rex Cooper with us on that December night who seemed to enjoy himself, chatting to the bishop who entered into the spirit of the evening with requests and knowledgeable discussion of jazz topics.

The other bishop involved in the gig world of Paul Donley was also Bishop Peter, Peter Smith, Roman Catholic bishop, at whose home we played for a priests' convocation. This was out at Poringland where in the grounds of the house was a huge marquee which would serve as a centre for all the food which was already being brought in by the caterers when we arrived at mid-morning. We were directed to a rather untidy stone gazebo at the back of the house which was to be our bandstand where, after linking up endless cable to some part of the house, we began our first session. The view was the back garden, dotted with ancient looking statues, and beyond to fields of grazing cattle who for the first hour seemed to be our sole audience.

The weather, being fine and sunny, albeit breezy, gave a meaning to our opening number – Irving Berlin's 'Blue Skies', followed by 'Shine'. Eventually, real people began to appear, obviously attracted by the strange sounds coming from the direction of the gazebo. I would have said that one in every three wore a white dog-collar as curiosity got the better of more and more who came to inspect this strange phenomenon of ancient gazebo with ancient musicians giving out ancient sounds. Some must have liked what they heard for they brought their plates of food and drink to sit in the garden and 'listen to the band'.

Unfortunately the weather began to deteriorate with the wind increasing sufficiently to blow my music away (here I jest, as it was the usual piece of paper listing quicks, slows, and no waltzes). It grew colder, while the rain, which had been showery, became heavy enough to drive the hardiest picnickers inside.

Eventually the afternoon dried with Bishop Peter's 'man' telling us that VIP Cardinal Hume and his entourage would be along shortly and would we play his favourite jazz number 'When the Saints Go Marching In'? (well, what else?!). We did so when he appeared with his escorts, and I hadn't realised how very tall he was, perhaps six feet four I'd say. He smiled in obvious pleasure and was then whisked off to I know not where, but not before Bishop Peter had shown his delight by indicating we should go to the canvas food hall.

I have never seen so many dog-collars gathered in one place as that afternoon at Poringland, and I don't recall a spread of food like it in all my years as a musician: whole salmon, chickens, hams, pies, bowls of salad, huge bowls of strawberries, gateaux, cheeses galore, and an endless line of smiling ladies in white pinnies persuading us to have something of everything until the plate could take no more, leaving us to stagger to a corner and enjoy it all.

The weather, seemingly taking a dislike to so many clerics, didn't improve much and we found quite a large gathering of them clustered round a television set in the bishop's lounge watching (I think) the FA Cup Final. Anyway, the 'God Bless You' variety of that gig was not without payment.

Pulham Market held an annual summer music festival with bands, groups and singers gathering there for entertainment on the village green in the day, and in the village hall and pubs in the evening. The whole thing seemed to be orchestrated (as they say these days) by a local retired doctor – Doctor Rawlence, known affectionately as 'Doc', a fine flute player who bordered on the eccentric and was charmingly vague.

Paul Donley was double-billed on these occasions, playing with the South Norfolk Symphonic Wind Band under their conductor Mike Booty and, of course, leading Yare Valley Jazz, which is where I came in.

The village green was packed with spectators, many with garden chairs, some with picnic tables, and all enjoying the beautiful day in such lovely surroundings.

Announcements came from someone on the church tower, while a television camera recorded some of the event. After the South Norfolk Band had pleased the crowd with popular music, it was the turn of 'Jazz on a Summer's Day' from Paul's hot-shots, perched precariously on a farm cart which seemed 'moved' by the music (sorry about that), giving the audience a taste of traditional swing main-stream.

We had various guest musicians such as Colin Bradfield, a wizard on the alto sax, and Gill Alexander in her familiar black fedora on bass for some of the time, while Tony Cleary may have been late, detained or planning his next barn conversion – you could never be sure which.

There were many other gigs with Paul for weddings and parties, all very carefree with a great deal of leg-pulling and laughter, both essential ingredients of what makes up a happy bunch of musicians playing something they enjoy and getting paid for it – sometimes!

CHAPTER THREE

Silver Threads Among the Gold

AMONG the many calls I had following my retirement was one from June Johnson, at that time in charge at the Essex Rooms Luncheon Club for the elderly, meeting daily in the church rooms in Essex Street in Norwich. June asked me if I would come and play the piano to these good folk on a Friday in return for a lunch and petrol money, to which I agreed readily. Thinking back, I'm not quite sure why a Friday: perhaps 'live' music to end off the week. I am always amused by an entertainment's announcement that so-and-so will be appearing 'live', which is either as opposed to 'dead' or that he or she may be distinguished from a cardboard cut-out. Mind you, some performers may give either of those impressions whilst I can remember several audiences that have appeared to be likewise.

That first performance or recital on that Friday opening I well remember as I played on an ancient upright which probably had its birth in the Victorian age, and had seen better days. Several members, noticing something was anew, eyed me curiously, possibly suspiciously, while others simply dozed, probably in customary fashion. Little by little the members realised I was playing the old piano properly, despite the fact that a few of the notes died on me even as I touched them, and a few smiles were raised with some attempts at singing. 'Hello, Hello, Who's Your Lady Friend', 'Oh You Beautiful Doll', and 'For Me and My Girl' seemed to please them, as well as others, and June was delighted. From then on I became a part of the Essex Rooms Club, making a lot of new friends, including a lovely lady from the north-east of England named Florrie Forde. Yes, Florrie Forde, who said that when she told people she was Florrie Forde they said to her, 'You can't be – she's dead'. Of course, Florrie had married a Mr Forde to give her her new identity which led to all the controversy. Adding to the arguments was the fact that Florrie Forde (of the Essex Rooms) was a fine pianist and, although not singing, was categorised under the heading of 'entertainer like the late Florrie Forde'.

Florrie would play the old German upright from 10am until I arrived to start, around 11.15am, which I would precede with a little chat to her, telling her we were both members of the Black and White Club. This was something I would remind her of each week when she would smile broadly and say, "I love playing the piano and I'm nearly 89. I've told my daughter – if I get to heaven and there is no piano there, I'm coming back again". She played a variety of things, but although she had the sheet music in front of her, she rarely used it, even for my requested favourite, 'Bacarolle, From The Tales of Hoffman'.

Gradually, my music began to fit in with the Friday scene at the Essex Rooms with my introduction of a mike and amplifier to not only announce things, but to encourage some of the club members to give the others the benefit of their vocal refrains. The one fly in the musical ointment was the wayward piano that craved so much attention, losing sound altogether near the top and having other notes playing completely out of tune. In its day it was no doubt a very fine instrument, for I have always maintained that whatever faults the Germans had in other things, they made the world's finest pianos, but by now the old monster clattered and wheezed its way through numbers which became torture to the ear.

Simon Cullum, piano doctor extraordinary, was sent for and, with stethoscope, scalpel and tuning fork, gave his diagnosis, declaring that the patient needed immediate treatment for a fee – Simon not being NHS. An operation was carried out, giving the old girl a new lease of life, although Dr Cullum did have to be summoned from time to time due to minor relapses.

Another doctor – Doctor Johnson of Litchfield fame – once said, 'Of all noises I think music the least disagreeable', which suggests he had had his ears assailed by some pop group or other of his day, though what he would have said about the Essex Rooms' clatter-box does not bear thinking about.

Simon Cullum was a wizard with pianos whom I had met in his official capacity tuning school instruments, and who came to tune my own dear Amyl (née Norwich Co-op) on a regular basis. His grandma, Elsie Beales, then aged about 98 and living at Foulger's House in Ber Street, Norwich, was entertaining the other residents with her piano hands almost daily.

I'm reminded here that I called for Simon's help with regard to my friend Catherine Soame-Hook's daughter who had bought a Baldwin piano which had developed playing faults. Catherine arranged for me to look at the said Baldwin (a famous American maker), and give my opinion. I found the top-end notes were all sticking, that is staying down and not returning, with the bass notes likewise.

Apparently, Catherine's daughter, having been dismayed by this, had demanded a visit from the vendor, who sent a young man who declared, "Yes, the notes do stick a little, but in any case the top and bottom end of the piano are hardly ever used!"

I could scarcely believe what he had said, as could not Simon Cullum later when making his assessment to suggest that the cost of correction would be high. As it was, Catherine being a very resolute and determined lady, rang the Baldwin piano company in New York who arranged a visit from their representative with the result that the ailing instrument was exchanged without hesitation for a new one for, like the Rolls Royce, a Baldwin 'never breaks down'.

Quite by chance into my life came Jimmy Skene who was to become a great musical friend until his death in 2000. The Taverham Singers were in a concert at Taverham High School, 'doubling' the bill with the Sillars Orchestra from Norwich, among whom was lead violin Jimmy Skene from Eaton. Eaton? I lived at Eaton but didn't know about Jimmy who, I later discovered, had lived at Chestnut Hill for thirteen years no less! Anyway, at the interval Paul, taking out his clarinet, said to me, "How about we liven up the start of the second half with some jazz ?" Jimmy, standing near, overhearing said, "May I join you? Swing fiddle – do you know 'Man I Love' in E flat ?" Yes, we certainly did.

I was stunned, Paul was stunned, and the audience incredulous. This little man, head bald, bespectacled, and looking like Mr Magoo, swinging into the number in a perfect facsimile of Stephane Grappelli. When 'Man I Love' finished, Jimmy, having extemporized his way through ten-thousand notes or more, the audience just roared their appreciation, demanding an encore to which we duly obliged with 'Sweet Georgia Brown'.

That evening, my first encounter with the brilliant Scot from Aberdeen was to be, as the song says, 'The Start of Something Big'. I invited him to join me on the Friday at the Essex Rooms which he seemed delighted to do, and there he discovered a wonderful rapport, a bond of friendship with just about every member. As for me, I had discovered a wonderful new friend, a superb musician who was to share the next few years with me in so many musical ventures.

Briefly, Jimmy Skene had been raised by musical parents, with gifted brothers and sisters, and had started his musical career on the violin in his home town of Aberdeen. Hardly out of short trousers, Jimmy was thrust into the world of the 'silent' cinema, with his father as leader in the beginning. He told me that the trio all had music, with the leader having a pedal which would turn the pages of everyone's music at the appropriate place, the leader keeping an eye on the screen.

One such leader had a reputation for both alcoholic over-indulgence and gimmickry. One slightly inebriated evening performance, with heroine Pearl White stranded, clinging to a cliff face, he struck up 'Charmaine' with the opening line, 'I wonder why you keep me waiting?' Jimmy said his typical musician's humour did not find amusement at management level.

At the showing of the silent version of *Moby Dick* our friend decided to lend some atmosphere to the scenes when, having purchased some whale blubber from Aberdeen dock, boiled it in a pot on a stove in the orchestra pit. The stench, permeating the whole cinema, was enough to make even the hardiest of Scots cover their noses as they hurriedly made their exit. Not surprisingly, Jimmy said, the management did not share the orchestra leader's attempt at realism, 'smellioscope' being well ahead of his time.

Jimmy made his own way in the musical world, beginning with his purchase of a trumpet which his father denounced as being a 'maker of noise' and not a musical instrument at all. Undeterred, Jimmy taught himself, very soon playing it in bands at the Beach Ballroom in his home town, and eventually making his way down to the 'big smoke' where he picked up gigs in Archer Street, the unofficial job centre for blowers, scrapers and bangers.

He played many summer seasons, including some memorable ones at the Palace Ballroom in Douglas on the Isle of Man. Jimmy became very well known for his playing of both trumpet and violin and for his pleasing personality, rubbing shoulders with the best musicians of the day in the 'Thirties.

After the war, in which he served as a musician (what else?), Jimmy joined as trumpet lead for a band on one of the luxury liners of the Union Castle Line, crossing to Johannesburg in three weeks with the reverse trip a further three weeks. This was in 1955, and the following year he was sent for by Mr Hubert Warren, the agent who booked bands for the shipping line, and was asked to form a band for the next trip. Jimmy hand-picked his men, playing music for coffee, church services, and dancing, over the Atlantic and back, something he was to do for the next twenty-one years until his retirement in 1977.

Chance brought him to live in Eaton, Norwich, which was where I entered his life story and he mine, albeit far too late. Each Friday I would collect him from Atmere Close where he lived with his daughter Pat and son-in-law David Philips, and on the way to the Essex Rooms he would recount to me stories of his life as an ocean-going band leader. There was the absent-minded captain with whom Jimmy sailed many a voyage, who could never remember Jimmy's surname.

"Now, Mr Skeet or Skeel, whatever your name is, we'll have 'Onward Christian Soldiers' for Sunday's service."

"But Captain, we had it last Sunday."

"No matter, we'll have it this Sunday, Mr Skeet."

"Yes Captain."

As a matter of fact, it was 'Onward Christian Soldiers' pretty well every Sunday, so much so that the orchestra stopped bothering with the music.

Once in Johannesburg, Jimmy was booked to play with the Jo'burg Symphony Orchestra with the invitation to quit sailing and be a permanent member, which was quite an honour since the JSO was world renowned.

During one such stay in Jo'burg, Jimmy fell within the clutches of a very wealthy South African widow who suggested our married matelot should make his future with her and live happily-ever-after in the shadow of Table Mountain. It must have all been very tempting with the idea of a wife in every port, this one dripping in diamonds and a fat cheque book to match, but no, there was wife Wilhelmina back in Aberdeen as well as the boys in the band. On both counts he declined: the Johannesburg Symphony and the rich widow. Gosh, what a man!

When I first met Jimmy he was mostly bald with a ring of hair around the ear and neck level which had to be 'trimmed' at a salon normally reserved for female beautification, costing him around £4.00. His baldness had been apparent many years before, even while he was at sea, which may have been exacerbated by ozone excess – I can't say.

One of his ship's bandsmen suggested he should try a wig, and on arrival in South Africa Jimmy bought himself a hair-piece which I believe he told me was ginger.

On returning to the *Windsor Castle* for the homeward voyage, the crew, including musicians had to muster for roll-call, with Jimmy sporting a head of hair. The aforementioned captain, coming down the line, reached Jimmy and asked: "Who the blazes are you?"

"Skene sir."

"You're nothing like him. I can always see Skeet's head."

"But I'm wearing..,"

"What's that on your head? If it is you, Skeet, come back looking normal."

However, Jimmy, rather daunted, persevered with the toupee – for a little while, anyway, despite the leg-pulling from fellow musicians and the curious looks from passengers. Then one day, as he strolled around the deck, a sudden gust caught the hair-piece, taking it out to the Atlantic where it bobbed on the water. It's likely that a passing ornithologist might have become quite excited, mistaking it for the nest of a red-breasted merganser or some other kind of sea bird. Anyway, it was back to being bald for James, and instant recognition by the crew and of course, the amnesiac and now seemingly myopic captain.

Further adventures of Jimmy will be described elsewhere in this book, but suffice to say here that he became a weekly feature at the Essex Rooms where he played his violin with me, displaying his professional skill at 'straight' and jazzy music.

The ageing piano tended to have bouts of sickness, with our valiant piano doctor – Simon Cultum – called in to administer medication, or even new bits, to make it work. Despite this, the music went on, with singing members adding their contribution: Eva Edwards who sang 'When You Wish Upon a Star', 'Somewhere My Love', and the theme from *Moulin Rouge*; and Bill Thurston who always added the touch of class with 'Floral Dance', 'Old Man River', and 'The Lost Chord'.

Then there was a real character called Jack Ali who half sang just about everything which meant just that: he knew half the words, improvising the rest with his own poetic rendition which I found more endearing than did some of the audience, and which made Jimmy fall about. At lunch table I would tell Jack Ali one or two jokes, which after lunch he would re-tell to the members. Unfortunately, he would completely forget the punch line, turning to me to ask, "What comes next Tony?", which does tend to take the edge off an otherwise funny story.

One of Jimmy's favourites was 'Little Sir Echo', when he would climb the stair to the gallery behind us and pretend to be my echo, yelling out 'Hello' in as many violinic ways as he could. I'm sure many of the listeners thought he and I were both due for a trip to a funny farm, but for the most part they took it in good humour – I think!

Came the time for June Johnson to retire, an emotional day with her daughter Petrina singing 'Pal Of My Cradle Days', the staff to bring out all the Kleenex tissues available, and the folks to worry and wonder about her successor. They need never have worried, for into the rôle stepped Shirley Leggett, whose husband Peter had once been a school pupil of mine, and at once she showed herself to be a very caring leader.

I ventured to broach the question of the piano, since it was becoming worse in its old age, too often in need of a call-out, with the bills ever rising, something the Luncheon Club could ill afford. Any acceptance of pianos from someone's granny or Aunt Maud was out of the question since all that meant was nursing unwanted cast-offs which generally sounded as though someone had dropped them down a mineshaft.

Shirley, seeing the nature of the problem, gave me the go-ahead to scan the local ads, not seeking out gems like, 'Piano: fair condition, would suit beginner, £30 ono'. That kind of piano would most certainly not suit a beginner but, on the contrary, any aspiring young Peter Katin or Eileen Joyce would be disillusioned in the extreme, if not for life. No, I had to consider modernity in the form of an electronic instrument, one that wouldn't need a piano doctor round every five minutes.

Now, no doubt there are those who would throw up their hands in horror at the thought of an electronic (or is it electric?) piano, but a new 'proper' piano, grand or upright, would cost the club a few bob, even with a whip round among the members. 'Technics elect. P'no with instruction book, hardly used, was new £1750, accept £650' read the advertisement, which I took to be was the piano, not the instruction book. The telephone code turned out to be Lowestoft and without further ado I consulted Shirley who thought she (well, not she personally), could come up with £500 but the remaining £150 would have to be borrowed from somewhere.

I decided to drive over to the Lowestoft address and see the Technics for myself, conscious of the fact that I had the promise of £500 but worried about a short-fall of £150. The lady vendor lived in an upstairs flat in a suburb of Lowestoft, surprisingly set among trees, with a large pond simply overcrowded with ducks and drakes. Mindfull of the fact that I might well have to make the descent from her apartment with a piano I trailed behind the lady, and her blind dog, to the sitting-room where stood the large black-coloured Technics. I sat playing it for a time, experimenting with buttons which produced a variety of sounds such as trumpet, sax, vibes, strings, organ and, would you believe – piano! It was quite obvious it would be just the thing for the Essex Rooms, and although there was no question of an offer (it was a great bargain anyway) I asked for first refusal, subject to the total cash sum being found. Jimmy Skene and I put our heads together, decided we would loan the £150 between us, and arrangements were made for Shirley's husband Peter and me to go down to Lowestoft in his van to collect the Technics. Fortunately, it came to pieces (not Peter's van) and he and I were able to transport the said piano back to Norwich with the minimum of trouble.

Once installed, the Technics became part of the furniture, being set in one corner opposite to that of the German upright which probably sulked until Florrie Forde played it each Friday morning from about 10am until it was our turn. You could say Florrie was the 'warm-up' act, playing tunes of yesteryear which delighted the early arrivals and gave Jimmy and me the chance for a chat over coffee.

I did invite Florrie to have a try on the electronic keyboard, but the poor lady, clearly terrified by the very idea, declined politely, saying that she knew nothing about new-fangled gadgets, much preferring the well-trusted piano (which was very far from well and not to be trusted).

The handbook, or manual, for Technics was just like most – written by someone in the early stages of a nightmare with no invitation to the reader to join him, until both become completely exasperated to the point of mental derangement. I did wonder if it would be possible to purchase a good translation into English, but decided on the trial and error method sans-manual. Passable sounds emerged, a satisfied look came over Jimmy's face and musical life remained at the Essex Rooms without a piano doctor in sight.

We would churn out selections from shows, including *White Horse Inn, Merry Widow, My Fair Lady, Sound of Music*, with Jimmy's favourite, *Memories of Ivor Novello*, as well as specialities for the violin such as *Schoen Rosmarin, Liebeslied* and *Liebesfreud* (all Kreisler) and Monti's *Czardas*. In the last names he would cheekily jump up and shout: 'Oi', much to everyone's amusement.

Of course, where ageing citizens are involved, you will have those who come and 'go', which meant that over a number of years there were many who would sing there no more and indeed, in the case of Florrie Forde, at 92, left 'her' precious piano at the Essex Rooms, and hopefully, joined one in heaven which I sincerely hope was in much better condition.

Jimmy decided to quit playing after about eight years, although he continued to come to the Essex Rooms, enjoying the friendship, the music and of course the lunches. The volunteer singers grew in numbers as an apparent wave of confidence swept through the luncheon club, invariably led by Barbara Smith who claimed never to have sung solo before.

However, what was needed was a really good singer, able to cover a big range of numbers, and with some charisma, but since the likes of Tony Bennett or Max Bygraves seemed to be fully booked, I had to look nearer to home.

Then along came Don – Don Hoffmann whom I had met singing with Madge Mildinhall's Singing Seniors, a strong voice and pleasing personality. Would he come to the Essex Rooms every other week? Of course he would, and from the very outset the members took to him and he to them. As well as standards, he would render Sinatra, Jolson, old-time, romantic waltzes, and ballads, but his favourite was Nat King Cole; indeed, had his daughter been a boy, she (he) would have been Nathaniel, but since she was not he gave her the nearest he could, calling her Natalie. On the funnier side, Don would give a superb impression of Gracie Fields with 'At The End of the Day' and 'Sally' in a most realistic high pitch that brought howls of laughter, especially when he gave the audience a cue line just before he sang it, which was how 'our Gracie' used to do it.

Don's wife Janet gave him a special birthday present of a radio mike and speaker which gave Don the freedom of the hall, and having no lead attached he could take it to anyone to give a song or part of a song, even those wheelchair members.

For eighteen months or more Don entertained the folk at the Essex Rooms, all the time building up a big repertoire, giving them his all, which everyone appreciated.

One Friday, after a typical great performance from him, I said my farewells to Don. 'See you next week', I called, leaving him chatting to some members who were awaiting their transport. At a nephew's birthday party in Kent the following evening, Don Hoffmann suffered a massive heart attack, collapsed and died, a huge shock to everyone, not least a distraught Janet and daughter Natalie.

The vacuum left at the Essex Rooms was never filled since there was no one of his panache and calibre. He sang to the people in a most engaging style. From my point of view he was a musician's singer, one you could follow with every one of his phrases, the slight pauses, the swinging endings and so on, and of course he was also a great guy.

Janet Hoffmann gave me the radio mike and speaker, for she said, "Don would have wanted you to have them."

Since then they have been used at the Essex Rooms every Friday where new faces have appeared, not only the members, but two of my musician friends agreed to come once a month to help entertain. Joe Dade, celebrated Norwich accordionist, came out of his subterranean home in the St Stephen's underpass to entertain with his varying repertoire which included a French selection, polkas, and the famous 'El Relicario'.

Joe, my great friend of many years, delighted everyone with his warm personality, his witty humour and his wonderful rapport with the old folk, some of whom were younger than he. He had a habit of making regular appearances in the *Eastern Evening News* with photographs depicting him as 'Accordionist Celebre' complete with striped shirt, neckerchief and beret, though mercifully sans-onions!

Bringing with him his guitar and his voice, along came Jimmy Beaumont for a once-a-month session, though not on the same Friday as Joe. Selections of Jolson, Fats Waller and the Singing Postman were included in Jim's repertoire, as well as attempting some accompaniment for the volunteer singers, who would often have a little difficulty with words or timing – or both. Jimmy, another friend of so many years, was a well-known Norwich musician who had played with many local bands, including Harry Sunderland's Delta Five, and the late Billy Duncan.

Behind the scenes at the Essex Rooms was a wonderful team led by Shirley Leggett and Pat Fuller, including cooks Pam Gould and Sarah Lake, helpers Olive Russell, Donna Barney, Tessa Nelson, Christine Parfitt, Christine Wilmer and Maureen Vogt.

We would arrange vocal solos from a fine singer called George Green with renderings of songs like 'The Way We Were' and 'Moonlight in Vermont'; Helen Smith with some typical Gracie Fields' or Sophie Tucker' numbers, and various contributions from Elsie Ashby and Brian Howard, the latter delighting everyone with his 'Ballad of Bethnal Green', by Paddy Roberts.

Olive Russell often blushed behind the mike with a song or two, while

'Dickie' Bird and David Williams obliged us with poetry readings thereby raising the cultural level to Oxbridge standards, or the BBC as we used to know it.

One of the members, Joe Fleisher, a wheelchair-bound ex-prisoner of war, has a perpetual grin which always broadens when I announce that 'Colonel Joe' has directed the whole Friday programme (which of course he hasn't, but it's a bit of fun just the same). It typifies the spirit of the club, just as an old couple did called Ernie and Hilda Dunn, he rendering his weekly song, utterly devoid of time and tune, and she giving us her regular contribution of a totally incomprehensible ditty in Shanghai Chinese.

Times change, folks come and go, but the Essex Rooms' luncheon clubs of this country will go on turning, urged on by the band of voluntary people who give their all to see to the welfare of people in the winter of their lives.

For all of them, life would be nothing without music, which is where I come in together with my good friends who see that everyone has a happy day with the music and fun, filling those brief hours, brightening their otherwise possibly dark lives.

31

CHAPTER FOUR

There's a Small Hotel

RECENTLY, I was reading of how you can have afternoon tea with full silver tea service, served by tail-coated waiters, at one of about six top London hotels, such as the Savoy or Ritz. To add elegance to this, a pianist will tinkle (the article's expression, not mine!) Cole Porter tunes on a grand piano behind a palm tree, not a customary location for a grand piano I felt.

All this will set you back a mere £27.00 per person, though the writer of the article did not reveal what it would cost without the pianist behind the palm tree, which one could only hazard a guess of around a fiver each. Pianists do not come cheaply.

One of the hotels offered three tea sessions: '1.30, 3.30 and 5.30 – booking in advance essential. At the 5.30 session is an optional bottle of champagne at £48.00', though I'm not sure if that included our palm tree and piano. A quick peep behind the palm tree would reveal that I was not at the Bechstein, even though I would dearly loved to have been.

As it was, I was continuing to play the creaking Evestaff at the Oaklands Hotel, a far cry from the Ritz Bechstein or the Savoy Steinway. From my vantage point in the lounge bar, I watched the customers having their pre-lunch aperitifs, although watching and playing at an upright isn't easy, tending to cause neck-ache. My music, together with the cigarette smoke, would drift over to the diners in the dining room, the division from the lounge being pillars and poles.

I watched too the changing of the managers, rather like the changing of the guard, for they seemed to come and go in rapid succession which was difficult to keep pace with. One of them, jolly George Wortley, I remember, always had time for a chat, mainly about football and I suppose by the frequency of the 'ins' and 'outs' of managers, he stayed a reasonably long time.

However, he too quit, summoned I believe to run a hotel in Southampton, and there followed a noticeable decline at the Oaklands, due, I would imagine, to a continuing change of staff and management, with mumblings of discontent among the patrons.

The 'regulars' would come and chat, request numbers or most importantly, buy me a drink. I jest here really, since it was never alcoholic (or alcofrolic as my late magician friend Harry Carson would say). One of them was Brian Redfern, known to some as Harry, who aspired to play cocktail piano, seeking my advice and tips each Sunday lunchtime. Brian had bought himself the latest thing in keyboards which he invited me to see at his home in Gordon Avenue. With the aid of commercial floppy disks, the machine, set up and looking like something I'd seen in Air Traffic Control, gave forth the most almighty sound of a twenty-five piece band playing Count Basie.

The Evestaff upright was becoming difficult to control, needing medical attention from time to time, which was a mere temporary repair until the next time the horrible sounds issued forth.

Of course it could be argued that it wouldn't make horrible sounds if it were not for me, but a dancing-school teacher friend, Janet Russen, said to me as she sipped her coffee, "Love the music Tony, shame about the piano."

That very week the Oaklands caught on fire, the lounge, bar and furnishings went up in smoke and, yes – the Evestaff upright. It hit the headlines in the local papers, whereupon I received two telephone calls: the first from the manager to tell me the tragic news, which meant I was out of work, and the second from Janet Russen who said, "Tony, I know I said the piano was bad, but there was no need to go to those lengths and try to burn the place down too!"

Arson? No one knew, but at least the sick old Evestaff was now dead and cremated and I did have the assurance of the manager that there would be a new piano. A new piano! He had said it – a new piano. New for old, perhaps, with the insurance coughing up enough for a Bechstein or a Steinway. What a thought! What joy! What rapture! The manager's blonde wife had 'always wanted a grand piano' and so, "a grand piano you shall have", he told her.

After eight weeks' absence from duty I received a telephone call to tell me that the hotel was almost refurbished, that things were back to normal, and that there was now a grand piano. Trying to contain my excitement, something hard to do where there is the prospect of meeting a grand piano face to face, I drove up to the hotel on the Sunday.

Do you ever have a sense that things are not quite what they should be, or there is a snag about to come and meet you? I remember that feeling I once had when I had booked a room in a French seaside resort on the understanding that the room was 'en face de la mer', only to discover that they had moved the sea and it was, in fact, 'en face de la cimetiere'!

The moment I stepped into the main entrance the snag feeling was there, which was soon to be announced by the manager, "Ah Tony...."

"You've got the new grand?"

"Well yes, but ..." (Now there's an expression to cast doubt, 'Yes but'; one that seems to be more and more prevalent, I find).

"You've had to send it back?"

"No-oo..."

"You've fallen behind with the payments and they've taken it back?" This I endeavoured to say in jocular fashion, naturally.

"It seems to need tuning...."

"Ah", I said which probably implied that not only did I know about such things but when given such an opinion by a non-musician generally has deeper significance. At first sight it was a beautiful-looking light-wood grand: an English Broadwood from around the first decade of the 20th century when it had been someone's pride and joy. I ran my fingers over the keys, the hotel manager looming in, his wife hovering expectantly. His suggestion that it needed tuning was about the biggest understatement I have ever heard, with the words 'overhauling', or 're-building' crossing my mind. On the positive side some notes actually played, but for the most part the rest were silent, stuck down, or made a noise like a bed spring, while a few, when played, copied the same pitch as the note next to it.

"I said it needed tuning", said the manager, "Do you know somebody?" How could I inflict such a cruelty on Simon Cullum? He would hate me forever, that was certain.

"I thought you said a *new* piano?" I said feebly.

"This one came from the hotel at Wroxham and had been kept in a cellar for three years, untouched. It was a bargain."

Oh dear, so that was it. Such 'bargains' are someone else's rubbish, invariably. Could I get a tuner quickly? Yes, I could. Could I manage today on the instrument? Well, I could try and I was hanged if I would go home minus pay.

That Sunday lunchtime recital will go down as one filled with quaint, cacophonous janglings, interspersed with clunks, bed spring noises and discords, accompanied by my hissed expletives, all of which could not have done much for my reputation. I might have qualified for some 'dep' work for Les Dawson at most.

To make matters worse, who should come into lunch but Peter Fenn, pianist friend, ex-Anglia TV 'Sale of the Century', etc. Of all the days!!

Seeing a 'distressed' piano in some distress with a distraught player, he came over to me with a most direct question.

"What the hell have you got there?"

Before I could deliver an adequate reply, Peter said, "If I were you I'd tell them to ***** it, and buzz off home."

Something along those lines had crossed my mind but, not wishing to cause offence nor lose my pay, I soldiered on.

When I'd finished at round 2.30pm two dear elderly ladies came over to express their thanks for the beautiful music, one of whom wore a deaf aid and I assumed the other to be completely tone deaf!

Piano surgeon Simon Cullum telephoned me on the Monday night with his first bulletin, to tell me he had been to the Oaklands all day and the best of a bad job was only half done.

"I've tuned half the notes", he said, "but the main problem is that the frame is cracked in three places."

"What does that imply?"

"It means that no matter how you try to tune a note it will still lose pitch because the peg cannot remain stable and stay in place."

"You mean it will go out of tune very quickly?"

"Yes, in a matter of days. The cracked frame cannot be repaired – the piano is a useless heap."

Simon dutifully returned the next day when he finished carrying out what he could, although one bass string which couldn't take it, broke and a replacement had to be ordered from London. You can say he'd made the best of a very bad job.

On the following Sunday, the manager confirmed that Simon had spent two full days on the piano, but his sole comment was one of grievance that it had cost him £52.00. My retort was 'that for two whole days' work I would have expected £152.00 and that he had got away with it lightly'.

Despite a couple more visits from Dr Cullum, that piano continued to lose pitch, making things very difficult for me and giving cause for some raised eyebrows from folk who clearly thought I was responsible for the bizarre outpourings.

There were those kind souls who, showing their obvious knowledge of such things, would murmur, "I think it needs tuning", but what it really needed was a Janet Russen to boom out for all to hear, "lovely music Tony – pity about the piano!"

Very soon the manager moved on, his wife too, with regrets at leaving behind her beloved grand, though as far as I was concerned she could have had it, and welcome.

The new manager said he knew nothing about pianos but appreciated that the Broadwood needed attention, though preferred to call in a consultant of his own, presumably for a second opinion – or third, if you counted mine. As it turned out, the doctor in question was Peter Holness who had formerly worked for Billy Willson at Willson's Music Shop and whom I knew to be an excellent tuner.

After his diagnosis, Peter presented the manager with a three page report about the piano, which he in turn showed to me. Before I even read it I knew what it would say: everything that Simon had reported, to the very last detail, although Peter hadn't actually written; 'It's a heap of rubbish'.

The governor's main worry was the item about 'the frame cracked in three places'.

"Could that mean it might break and the whole weight of it fall and crack the floor?"

"No", I reassured him. "What it does mean is that due to the cracked condition of the frame, the tuning pegs will never hold and the piano will stay out of tune – permanently."

I had bought a new electric (electronic!) piano – a Roland FP1 with a fully-weighted keyboard that if carried about, would be a guarantee to a hernia, if not a double. Against that it was a beautiful keyboard, full concert grand length (I do mean just the keyboard) with a powerful sound, ideal for cocktail lounges.

The nervous manager had no objection to my bringing Roland, especially after being told that the cost of rebuilding the Broadwood would be around £4,000. I needed anti-hernia equipment, so invested in a sack-barrow which fitted in the car and on the Sunday, set up in the Oaklands' lounge.

It set a bizarre scene really: a great monster of a grand piano standing by, whilst I played on an electric grand alongside. The sound seemed to rouse and captivate the diners and I have to say appeared to lift the atmosphere there since at the time the hotel was going through troubled waters which had certainly filtered through to the patrons.

Naturally there were those who ventured to enquire why the Broadwood was standing idle, those who thought I had taken exception to it and those who had seen nothing amiss with it in the first place, although I should imagine the last-named group was probably of the tone deaf variety.

We had some regular patrons who became familiar, friendly faces, such as Jerry Masters and his lady friend Monica, she always asking for 'Poor Butterfly', and he my Fats Waller medley. This would include 'My Very Good Friend The Milkman', 'When Somebody Thinks You're Wonderful', 'I'm Gonna Sit Right Down and Write Myself a Letter' and of course 'Ain't Misbehavin'.

It was around this time that I really got to know Peter Fenn and his lovely wife Shirley who became regular visitors for Sunday lunch. The reader will appreciate that pianists rarely meet and for the most part he had been a name to me and vice versa. Peter admired Roland greatly, making enquiries from

Allen's of Great Yarmouth if it was available, but learning to his disappointment that it was now obsolete. However, you can say that through music our friendship grew ever thus to the present day.

Our nervous manager departed, heads dropped and things at the Oaklands did not look good although, surprisingly enough, nobody suggested I leave which I suppose meant I had been 'giving satisfaction'.

Late in the 'Nineties came Mr Michael Piercy and his wife Toni to buy – yes, buy – the Oaklands. I had seen over a dozen managers arrive and depart in my time but this was different – a new owner, perhaps to make sweeping changes like sweeping me out of the door.

"You stay", said Mr Piercy, "You're good."

And so, stay I did, although I had exchanged mighty Roland for a comparatively lightweight Technics which carried a wealth of rhythms and voices, putting me into the technical class of keyboard players.

Mr Piercy asked me what he should do about the Broadwood and totally resisting the temptation of an ungentlemanly answer, suggested he sent it for auction, where it might be snapped up by an enthusiast, or an idiot.

'There's a small hotel' says the Rodgers and Hart classic, though nowadays the Oaklands could hardly be classed as small having been extended considerably by the go-ahead Mr Piercy.

The hotel is as busy as it has ever been and I am pleased to have given the customers my music each Sunday, meeting so many delightful people along the way.

CHAPTER FIVE

Dance Little Lady

NOEL Coward's song 'Don't Put Your Daughter On The Stage Mrs Worthington' seemed to jump off the pages as I started out on my career as dancing school pianist/accompanist with the academy run by Judy Habbitts.

There were hordes of pink girls, all dressed alike, squealing and waving arms about, running around like demented chickens. As I took my place at the Zender upright at the Notre Dame Prep School, waiting for instructions from Madame, I was clearly not the Mother Hen and really wondered what I was doing there in the first place. A clap of the hands, the instruction: "Quiet!" and we went straight into the routines of nursery rhymes that baptized four or five year olds – which is what they were.

Actually, I was a little rusty on my nursery rhymes, not surprising really after fifty years or more, and some I really couldn't remember, for which I was loudly chastised by Mrs Habbitts.

"Surely you must know 'I Love Little Pussy', Tony!"

Well, recalling my days in the dance band world I would have said that it was a number which was not often requested, though of course it must have been among those songs sung to my daughter Elisabeth. 'Here We Go Round The Mulberry Bush' was simple enough being a plagiarized 'Nuts in May' from the Paul Jones era, and 'Ring a Ring O' Roses' was always a winner with my splendid glissando down the keys as 'we all fall down'. As the afternoon progressed the girls grew taller and we moved on to ballet with knee bends, hand ripples and springs in first (the girls, not me).

Since the music had no speed directives either in Italian or English I had no idea what tempo to use, which invariably meant I was either too fast or too slow, but rarely correct.

In the standards that followed I was playing in French which made it harder with things like demi-plies, changements, porte temps leve and petits jetes, all of which appeared to come as second nature to the girls who performed them beautifully.

The senior set must have studied at the Paris Sorbonne since their very advanced ballet sequences included battements tendus, assembles souterns, echappes sauté and port de bras, which seemed easy to them, as if French were their native language. The set music was about as interesting as the old TV test card, musically speaking, correct but so, so dull.

Looking back at the afternoons at Notre Dame School I suppose I enjoyed learning about dance accompaniment. The East German-made piano, although a bit clinical, wasn't bad but I just wish I'd had better acknowledgement of my professional musician status at times.

Came the day I completed my apprenticeship at the Notre Dame School and was promoted to Judy's headquarters at the Bob Carter Centre, Drayton, though of course as probationer pianist not yet fully accomplished at his nursery rhymes.

It was there I joined the illustrious ranks of dancing pianists: that is to say, pianists who played for dancing, not actually doing the dancing, though thinking about it we did dance on strings for Mrs Habbitts.

You aimed to get a first-class certificate which entailed playing anything and everything at Judy's nod, stopping at another nod, not stopping at what you thought was a nod, and at the same time watching her feet. Added to this, you had to blu-tack posters (hundreds of them) in the foyer, tie little tots' shoe-laces, get groups of children into circles and all the while you played the six out of ten upright – quietly.

All the while this was going on, at the end of the room was an audience of adoring mothers, grandmothers, aunts and occasional male persons, many of whom would give 'Oliver Hardy' waves to their darlings and looks of sympathetic pity in my direction. The latter was due to the numerous verbal castigations that came my way when I mistook a nod, played too loudly, too softly, too slowly, too quickly, too early, too late or all of these at the same time, thus showing what an inadequate dancing pianist sounded like and after all, a probationer.

Other ranks of accompanists, presumably fully qualified, were Sally, Mary Bettany and a retired clergyman called Ronald who might have been the dancing schools' chaplain for all I know, but although much more highly qualified than I, did, I understand get even more 'flak' than I on occasions. Some nervous grandmas even shed tears, so they said.

The little ones went through 'story' dancing with Judy with trips to the park, the garden, the zoo, and the seaside with suitable music supplied by yours truly, after which we went into nursery rhyme routine. These I listed with keys and starting notes which I had copied from a nursery rhyme album by Mary Barham-Johnson that proved an invaluable help. I was absolutely superb at 'Humpty Dumpty', reasonably good with my 'Hickory Dickory Dock', passably so with 'Mary Mary Quite Contrary' but unsure of myself with 'Baa Baa Blacksheep', often confusing it with 'Twinkle Twinkle Little Star'. However, I understand this was often the case with even the top players.

"You mean to say you don't know 'Postman Pat'?" said Judy.

"Girls – Mr Ireland doesn't know 'Postman Pat'!"

It was appalling; they were obviously shocked and I ought to have felt quite ashamed, although I did wonder what the reaction would have been had the admonition been put to, say Alfred Brendel or Oscar Peterson and whether 'Postman Pat' featured in their respective repertoires.

For myself, I was more a 'Magic Roundabout' man, having a thing about Zebedee and Ermyntrude, although prior to writing this book would never have revealed it to anyone!

Instead of telling me to write out one hundred times: "I must learn to play Postman Pat", Judy said, "I'll get Mary to send you a copy", though failing to add ,'in a plain wrapper'.

After the final nursery rhyme where all of them gathered round the piano perhaps to sing 'Little Miss Muffet' (this is the same as 'Little Jack Horner' – the tune, that is) they all got up, curtsied stiffly and chorused: "Thank you". They all ran off to gran/mum/aunt or A N Other whilst the next pink horde scampered in to do similar routines.

There seemed to be dozens of these tiny pink females, all shapes and sizes, with high-pitched voices and an urge to run all over the room. Some of them decided to cry loudly or run off to granny or mummy despite Judy's attempts to retain them, but most formed up in a sort of circle to start with everybody's favourite, 'Mulberry Bush'. Perhaps a manual should be published entitled *A Musician's Guide to Nursery Rhymes* since to the uneducated they tend to sound all alike.

As the afternoon progressed the girls grew bigger, by which of course I mean that older classes came in to perform – tap and something called 'Modern', though not to nursery rhymes.

Tap began with some warm up to 'Spring Spring Spring' which was straight out of showtime stuff, all very enjoyable once I got the tempo right, directed by Judy. Then it was to the barre, which sounded like a familiar invitation to musicians but was, in reality, working at handrails for things like shuffles and cramp rolls, where I played 'The Old Soft Shoe' and 'Yellow Rose of Texas'.

I was introduced to that world of spring hops, pick-up steps, step heal beats and amalgamations as I busked my way through 'thirties and 'forties standards which fitted beautifully. It crossed my mind that the youngsters were dancing to numbers their grandparents knew, tunes that were unknown to them, mainly because radio and television had filed them under 'buried and not for resurrection'.

The tap routines were very good, precise and neat, every girl (and the occasional boy) putting their all into it, the dozens of tap shoes sounding as one (pair, that is). To my untrained eye and ear 'Modern' seemed rather like gymnastics set to music with things like side kicks and split runs, the latter consisting of girls charging full stride from one corner of the hall to the other, though quite what it had to do with dancing was something of a mystery to me. At a given moment the girls would give their curtsy and thanks, while I was relieved by the faithful Mary to take over the ailing upright to play for dozens more aspiring Margot Fonteyns.

Saturday morning classes with Donna Smith started at Harwood Road in the church hall of St John's, Lakenham. Girls of all shapes, sizes and ages did ballet, tap and modern, whilst I struggled on an upright of uncertain vintage and balance, following them as best I could. The custodians of the hall, to their credit, kept the piano locked with an obvious eye to potential vandalism. As I recall, it was one of those pianos that had been made taller by excessively high wheels which meant that when you were seated at it, your nose was on a level with the keyboard. It reminded me of cars where the driver sits so low he's looking at the road through the steering wheel.

There are degrees of vandalism to pianos, for apart from out and out wilful scratching of woodwork, breaking of keys and strings, or ripping the music stand, there is the vandalism of standing beer glasses, tea or coffee cups on it, wine bottles, beer bottles, ash trays and so on and so forth. At the Bob Carter Centre the items 'dumped' on the top of the upright were keys, ballet shoes, brooches, watches, necklaces, jumpers, ribbons, laces and sweets, all of which I would remove and place elsewhere. It never ceases to amaze me how people will cosset their furniture, from cabinets to sideboards, from tables to tall-boys, but pianos are just there as depositories for anything and children are literally given the freedom of the keyboard. Just imagine it from the piano's point of view! "Oh no, here come those kids again. What are they going to do this time?"

At the Hewett School was a lovely grand – or at least it had been until somebody removed the screws from the hinges to the lid so that the whole thing moved about and wouldn't stay up or close properly. Why do they do it?

At Thorpe Hamlet was a vintage Lipp grand with people's names scratched all over it until the well-meaning school caretaker painted the instrument black and put huge wheels on it which would make the performer play it at nose level.

Pianos, like people, are born in mint, pristine condition and are ruined by human-kind; age has nothing to with it for if they are looked after well they can be advertised 'as new', though I can't be totally sure about people in this respect.

When Donna left the Harwood Road hall we took up residence (if that is the correct expression) at St Mark's Church Hall on City Road. There I found a piano that had been abused dreadfully, for not only were most of its notes dead and disfigured, some maniac had severed its loud pedal. As I recall, I struggled valiantly that Saturday, attempting to play recognizable tunes on about a dozen and a half notes, all of which cried out to be tuned or else put down. With all due respect to the dear upright I had to take along my Casio the following week, playing for the young dancers with my back to it, hardly daring to look at the poor thing.

Shortly after this we all moved to St Alban's Hall in Grove Walk, a bright and airy room with a monster of an upright piano on the rather high stage, something I'm not fond of, to be so far away from the audience, or in this case, the young dancers. As to the piano itself I would have given it a high mark out of ten except for the fact that some of the notes were arthritic and two had severe paralysis, unable to move at all. Those with arthritics could be depressed but refuse to come up again, a phenomenon experienced by many a pianist, though perhaps not at the Albert Hall. There were a considerable number of these keys and I spent the time playing, watching the dancers, listening for Donna's instructions, while at the same time frantically retrieving sunken keys which must have given the impression to any onlooker of a demented pianist fighting mosquitoes or hornets.

I made some enquiries as to the possibility of treatment, or even rehabilitation, for the piano but was informed that 'experts' who had been called in could offer no cure, though how it got into that condition in the first place defies explanation.

They were very happy Saturday sessions with Donna Smith's dancing school and when I decided to make my exit, she presented me with a volume of *Grove's Dictionary of Music*, a most generous gesture.

The Leney family I had known for a considerable time, dating back to when Dr Peter Leney came as a locum to my house in Valleyside Road to examine me after my back had succumbed to lifting two and a half tons of Westmoreland stone for a rock garden. Added to this was a further two and half tons of Cotswold stone for a dry stone wall, not that I attempted to lift it all in one go you understand, but nevertheless the effort had caused me to give the impression of a palaeanthropic man, unable to be homo erectus. From the bedroom window Dr Leney observed my handiwork from which he was able to establish the cause of my vertebral pain, as he asked:

"Did you do all that?"

"Most of it."

"Then I'm not surprised you're in the state you are!"

He handed my wife Jane a prescription which she took, not to a chemist but to a local timber merchant for two planks of wood for me to lie on, which were to be the basis of my bed for the weeks to come.

Peter and Carla Leney had three children whom they wisely sent to Thorpe Hamlet school, although it has to be said they did live in Thorpe which was in the catchment area.

John, the eldest, took up the drums which was not really surprising since his father spent part of his life being a drummer in a jazz group where the pianist was a great friend of mine: David Morgan. It wouldn't have surprised me at all if their signature tune had been 'Doctor Jazz'!

John's brother Richard became a very good trumpet player, learning his skills from Barry Mason at Thorpe Hamlet school, to become a pro after leaving school and joining the modern version of 'Geraldo's Navy', by which I mean a cruise musician.

Alison Leney played the alto sax in the school orchestra and jazz band and continued to play after she left the school. Why, in this chapter about dancing schools, am I giving a potted history of the Leney family? Simply because Carla Leney, wife and mother, ran the Carla Leney School of Dance, and it was quite early in my retirement from teaching that she asked me to go along to her studio to play for the 'little ones'. Carla had directed me down Duke Street in Norwich to a big white building on the left where there was a large sign which read: 'St Mary's Works'.

Such notices often arouse a perverted urge in me to scribble something underneath and for this one I would dearly have loved to add: 'Why not try it for yourself?'.

I suspect this must be part of the quaint humour associated with musicians' but if I see a fly sheet that shows some ambiguity I'm sorely tempted to add my sub-heading. On one such poster outside Poringland Stores it read: 'Free Big Mac', to which I yearned to add: 'Protest forms in shop'.

On our little wooden 'bus shelter' I'd love to paste 'Under Offer' and I actually passed a farm where the farmer had put out a sign: 'Potatoes', under which some Francophile wag had printed: 'Twinned with Pommes de Terre'. Such things used to appear in the rear windows of cars, some of which were very funny, but the wittiest I ever saw was the one that read: 'If you can read this, then someone's pinched my caravan'.

I found Carla in an upstair room with lots of windows, barres round the walls, a slidy bouncy floor and an upright that had been tuned, together with two books of nursery rhymes, one of them American.

After we had renewed our acquaintances, Carla briefed me on what 'dances' the little ones would do and mums with toddlers came in, all very shy, which included many mums. When they had kissed their prodigies, the mothers went out leaving Carla to take the young dancers through their routines which were similar to what I'd done before with the other schools.

As with the others, there were youngsters who would suddenly cry, or run out, or leak on the floor, but it was all part of the course, as they say.

After the class had gone, Carla and I would talk over a cup of coffee, reminiscing about life as we remembered it at Thorpe Hamlet school or generally putting the world to rights (or some of it) and end the afternoon session on a very pleasant and happy note. Some of the dance teachers put on shows with, as the song from *Mack and Mabel* says 'Hundreds of Girls'. It was not only a chance for the school to show off what they could do but also for hundreds of mums and grandmas to go: "Ah", clap wildly and shed tears, often at the same time.

Apart from the occasional run-through at classes, pianists were not involved, since all the music was on tape, which hardly helps the musicians' cri de coeur 'Keep music live'. Keeping the hundreds of girls (and a few boys) in some kind of order, on and off stage, must have been quite an ordeal and the tales of wrong exits and entries, of crying and running off are legion.

I was told recently of a little girl at the end of a show, who was unable to locate her mummy and was asked: "What's your mummy's name?"

A negative shake of head.

"What is she wearing?"

A further nod.

"What is she like – can you describe her?"

The infant replied, "Big tits!"

Most succinct.

Rules are rules, so they say, and the various schools and academies stipulated that all dance examinations should be accompanied by a 'live' pianist on (presumably) a 'live' piano, at which point I ought to say: "Hurrah – keep music live." Since I understand that this rule has now been relaxed with tapes allowed, I won't say it.

My services as a 'live' exam pianist have been called upon many times by a long list of dance teachers including Judy Habbitts, Donna Smith, Carla Leney, Judith Fox, Janet Russen and Peggy Carr – quite impressive.

Having had more than my share of music examiners when I was head of music at Thorpe Hamlet, I was fully prepared for the assortment of dance examiners that I was to meet. Did I say fully prepared? Well, hardly, for in more than one instance I felt I was definitely intruding in a female-dominated domain and should certainly have been wearing a skirt.

You could see the look: 'It's a man – what's he doing here? We always have a woman pianist...' Some others thought I should blend in with the wallpaper, while others thought I WAS the wallpaper. In other words, the pianist was an irritating necessity, particularly one of the male variety who really had no business being there at all.

During some of the exams I played for I felt like a naughty boy being scolded for playing too fast, too slow, too loud, too soft while there were those ladies who objected to my having coffee in the same room and in one case I had to withdraw to the kitchen to eat. What of the pianos?

Well, I've already mentioned the Drayton and the St Mary uprights and there was a reasonable one at Loddon, but the best of the lot was Janet Russen's Bechstein at the Dell at Wagon and Horses Lane. It was a beauty with so much power in the bass you could hear it halfway down Magdalen Street: an absolute joy to play.

Since beginning this book, sadly I have learned of the death of the lovely Janet Russen, a superb teacher of dance and loved by so many people.

Playing for dancing schools was quite an experience, for it is an acquired skill ranging from tiny tots' nursery rhyme through to ballet, tap and modern, and I learned the discipline of it all which goes to make the dancers (male and female) into self-assured people, having good poise and deportment.

The late and lamented Roy Castle, himself a most talented musician and dancer, used to sing about dedication, the key to coming out top in what you do, something I witnessed so much of in my interesting career as dancing school accompanist, where so much talent often abounded.

CHAPTER SIX

Keep Young and Beautiful

A T Avenue Road school in those war years I remember PT lessons as they were then called. Physical Training, which when I became a teacher was known as PE (Physical Education), was conducted in the school playground with boys and girls changing into gym shoes and nothing more. By this I mean, of course, we didn't change into full PT kit, but faced the teacher doing things like 'bend and stretch', 'running or jumping on the spot' and 'touching your toes' – with no bent knees, mind! Several boys, including me, at the back, were discreetly bending their knees when there came a stern voice from behind:

"Anthony Ireland, you're bending your knees."

It was the fearsome Mrs Hughes, the headmistress, checking on the movements of those who thought they were safe from the teacher's gaze.

The sessions were held in the playground in fine weather, something I mention because in later years on a teaching practice at a senior school in Feltham I saw a squad of boys doing PT in the pouring rain, instructed by the form master wearing a mackintosh and carrying a large black umbrella!

At Avenue Road when it was wet, we had PT in the hall with something called music and movement, with either music from the gramophone or occasionally Mrs Hughes at the piano, who had the remarkable and enviable facility of playing and watching you at the same time.

She would often spot me (and others) larking about . . . what you? Yes, indeed: angelic Anthony assing around, who would be severely reprimanded and told that Music and Movement was a serious business, not a time for clowning.

Music and Movement! A forerunner of my role to come as a pianist for 'Keep Fit', in the first instance in the capable hands of Frances Chaplin.

I remembered the radio 'Keep Fit' programmes with Eileen Fowler: "And we're going to bend from the waist to touch our toes today: and a – one, two, three..", by which time her pianist was there with her into a steady 3/4 number, sometimes a familiar tune.

To a school-boy it all sounded rather boring, but I do recall my fascination with the pianist's ability to follow exactly, which I suppose I called to mind as I first worked for Frances.

The venue was Heather Avenue school at Hellesdon in the assembly hall where I found Frances dressed in a colourful leotard ready for the 'off'". There was the whitewood Kemble upright, so beloved by NAAFIs, Sergeants' messes and education authorities, presumably to withstand the rigours in each case, from rough perambulations to quack piano players, for they were built minus any aestheticism to combat every misuse or abuse.

Bechsteins, Steinways and their ilk are instruments of joy, bringing a broad smile to any pianist's face just to look at them, whereas their probable reaction at seeing a Kemble would be: 'Oh, for crying out loud', or words to that effect.

The ladies of the Keep Fit class arrived, were introduced to the newest keyboard phenomenum and promptly launched into various step exercises, mainly in fox-trot time to tunes of yesteryear.

To break the monotony for everyone, not least of all me, we would change to 3/4 time, tango rhythm or, the favourite of Frances, the cha-cha to the Norman Petty tune 'Wheels'. It was hard work on the Kemble but on the whole a jolly time, with a small raffle and some applause for me which is always gratifying, even though I was being paid. The ladies themselves, varying in size and attire, were exercising to try and correct any disproportion they had incurred over a period of time, and under the watchful eye of the affable Frances, would hopefully achieve such a feat.

Frances had a friend called Betty Phillp who did the same kind of Keep Fit classes, based at the Hewett School in Norwich, where she was employed by Norwich Adult Education. Like Frances, Betty hated taped music (quite right too), much preferring to have the 'live' variety or pianist which in most cases amounts to the same thing.

So it was that I had a telephone call from Betty Phillp who had been given my name by Frances and would I like to play for her and her ladies on Monday nights? Having agreed terms and conditions, as they say, I went along to the Hewett School to meet Betty, a delightful and vivacious lady dressed in a sparkly leotard which gave the impression of her having silver painted legs.

As the members of the class came in, Betty greeted each one and very soon the big hall seemed to be swarming with her 'ladies', almost all attired in colourful leotards which made me think that had Monsieur Leotard been alive, he would have made quite a packet on the sales of his invention.

The only differences between Betty's class and that of Frances were that the average age of the former was slightly lower and there were a lot more of them. In the corner of the hall stood a light-brown grand, a Bechstein no less but one that came into the category of severe misuse and abuse, presumably perpetrated by imbeciles. The lid hinges had been unscrewed so that the lid simply lay on the top which meant it couldn't be raised. Scratchings were everywhere and the poor thing was in desperate need of a piano doctor, with tuning a priority.

When any piano is out of sorts, I'm always worried that listeners should conclude that I (the pianist) am responsible for the unusual sounds issuing forth but the Hewett Bechstein was so badly out of tune that the majority of the Keep Fit ladies expressed sympathy with me. The head of heads to whom Betty had to make obeisance said that there were difficulties involved over the question of tuning the piano, or in other words miles of red tape had to be wound before anything could be done, plus the inevitable subject of who would pay.

Betty's 'warming up' was fast and furious exercises to what I would term 'quicksteps' which I reeled off in a non-stop medley of about fifteen minutes. I would include many old favourites such as 'Blue Skies', 'Who's Sorry Now?', 'Somebody Loves Me' and of course 'S'Wonderful', all written before any of the ladies were born and come to think of it, I also.

The rest of Betty's programme included a set of sequenced routines such as one involving a good deal of 'kicking' like Tiller girls to numbers like 'Mame' or 'Hello Dolly', both by Jerry Herman. These were most enjoyable for me since it was like playing for some sort of variety show dancers with the music fitting the movements so well, all devised by the dynamic Betty Philip. Other routines were floor work and exercises in tango rhythm which Betty loved.

"Tango, Tony", she would say, whereupon I would launch into Leroy Anderson's 'Blue Tango' or 'La Cumparsita', although her particular favourite was 'Perhaps, Perhaps, Perhaps'.

The one and half hours would end with a 'slow numbers' routine where I used romantic music like 'Misty' or Betty's favourite song 'Moonlight in Vermont', the final number which would bring applause from the 'girls'.

Betty had big classes with the names too numerous to mention but one of them, Carol, would organise extramural things like a Christmas dinner, to which I was always invited.

At the first dinner, held at 'The Cock' at Lakenham, I walked in to find twenty-five to thirty of the class all dressed in their best, almost totally unrecognisable. My big faux-pas was to say how lovely I thought they all looked with their clothes on!

The landlord, who had witnessed my greeting them all, asked in jocular fashion:

"Do they all belong to you?"

"But of course."

"Well lucky you", he retorted, "I've got just the one and she's enough for any man!"

Doubtless he mistook me for a member (or even leader) of some sect or other that permits polygamy, assuming that they were all my concubines.

During the ten years I spent with Betty Phillp and her ladies I got to know many of them, hearing about their lives, their families, their ups-and-downs, particularly when Betty would have an 'end of term' get-together at her home.

A delightful lady called Cynthia Fisher got in touch with me to ask if I would play for something called 'Extend' which I understood was a sit and stand form of 'Keep Fit' for ladies (and gentlemen) who didn't qualify for aerobics any longer.

I agreed to go along to the Eaton Parish Hall, on Colman Road in Norwich, every Thursday morning to supply the musical bit on the resident upright.

Cynthia Fisher, who looked remarkably under-age for retirement was quite charming. She kept herself fit by a daily round of golf, while twice a week ran an Extend group, one at Brundall and the other at Colman Road.

She was very knowledgeable about her music, favouring the old and trusted evergreens of the 'thirties and 'forties, of which she seemed to know all the words. Her special favourites were 'Once in a While' and 'Makin' Whoopee', the latter being a highly suitable number for forceful exercises.

As to the resident upright, there are a number of epithets which came to mind at the time such as cacophonous, tuneless and appalling, all of which were no fault of the poor, wretched piano which had no doubt been almost bashed senseless by half-wits in search of monkey music.

It was so bad that what you played at the top half of the keyboard bore no resemblance to that in the middle, with the bass just doing its own thing. To add to the misery of it all, the music stand was broken, one of the support pegs missing (presumably taken by an avid collector), and there was no stool. Something needed to be done and done urgently which led me to leave a note on the piano requesting it to be tuned as soon as possible (the piano, not the note – though it could have been several notes!).

The following week, the hall secretary appeared to tell me that the tuner was not due for another two months, which is rather like informing the owner of a broken down car that his service isn't due yet. My suggestion was to ask the tuner to come ahead of schedule, something totally unheard of apparently but nevertheless he complied, amazingly enough.

During the next few weeks, the tuner left messages to the effect he would have to return to make corrections, that the broken tops of certain keys were glued and shouldn't be touched and that a few felts and hammers needed attention.

Frankly, I'd have preferred he returned with either an axe or a large van to take it away, for despite all his visitations, the poor old thing grew worse, though I did take my own stool.

There were half-hearted promises that a replacement was forthcoming, that a lady of the parish had left a piano in her legacy and so on, which all seemed to be murmurings in the wind.

However, I arrived one Thursday to be told:

"There's a new piano."

A new piano! A new piano?

Well, no – the old brown heap was gone certainly and in its place what appeared to be a new black heap, which it turned out had been given by a lady who didn't want it any more. When I played it I wasn't surprised and – guess what? It needed tuning and, no, there was no stool!

'The show must go on' is the old theatrical saying and so it did with my accompanying Cynthia Fisher's Extend until she announced her retirement, following a small heart attack and her preference for golf.

Did I know anybody who could, or would take over?

Well, yes I did: Frances Chaplin, no less, and before long she was in charge at Colman Road with me at the piano, the old partnership from Heather Avenue back in business.

Of course, Cynthia Fisher was a hard act to follow but Frances took up the challenge, maybe a shade too vigorously for some, who couldn't keep it up, although I managed well enough. Interestingly, there were some of the male variety in the Colman Road classes, unlike Betty's where it was 'Put Me Among the Girls'.

Ironically enough, I had retired from working life as a teacher employed by Norfolk County Council but for both the Hewett and Eaton Keep Fit brigades I was in their employ again, taxed moreover, so was unable to offer either of them 'cut price for cash'.

Both Betty and Frances ran well-disciplined classes which responded well to their demands and I would marvel at the step work which compared favourably with any modern line dancing. It was an enjoyable experience for me that I would have been sorry to miss even though merely watching them all from my piano stool, sometimes left me exhausted.

CHAPTER SEVEN

Another Op'ning, Another Show

THE telephone was forever ringing, which in a way was a good thing, a comforting thought that not only did people believe I was still alive, but actually wanted my services – as a pianist, you understand. A regular caller was Paul Donley who would come up with some incredible gig or other in the most outlandish places. It would never have surprised me if he had been booked to play at the top of Ben Nevis or on a North Sea trawler or even for the Wormwood Scrubs Christmas bun fight. One evening, early in 1990 he telephoned: "How do you fancy playing for a show – a musical?"

"Go on."

"It's a group called the 'Ad Hocs' from Hethersett and Wymondham: a lady called Wendy Nichols."

"Oh yes; and the show?"

"*The Boy Friend.*"

That very show was enough to make me more than interested, for as a very young man my parents and I had gone to Oxford on a visit to my brother David, then at Brasenose reading law. Sparing no expense, my father ordered dinner at the Randolph, after which we went to the theatre where Sandy Wilson's clever musical, a pastiche send-up of the 'Twenties was having its pre-London run. I loved every moment, knowing that the success of *The Boy Friend* was almost certain and on returning home I bought the piano selection from Willson's (no relation) Music Bazaar for three shillings and sixpence.

Many of the songs I could play without music including 'It's Never Too Late to Fall in Love', 'I Could be Happy with You' and 'The Boy Friend' so Paul Donley's question: "How do you fancy playing for a musical?" had to be answered in the affirmative.

We gathered in the comfort of Roger Garrard's home to meet the members of the 'Ad Hocs', Roger being their producer and hosting the cast for the auditions.

Paul gave them a 'warming up' routine of scales and arpeggios, after which we launched into some of the numbers in 'The Boy Friend' from the many vocal scores that were there. For me it was highly enjoyable, playing the numbers I knew well, with others not so familiar and I knew I was going to enjoy this production, particularly since it seemed the ideal tonic I needed to lift my spirits.

It's difficult to remember how the members of the cast were chosen for the parts, presumably by audition with Roger Garrard the producer and Paul Donley the musical director, but the lead fell to Wendy Nichols to play Polly Brown with Tony being played by Lloyd Parfitt. Other members of the Ad Hocs whom I was to get to know well in the years to follow were Royle Drew, Ian 'Oz' Topliff, Nora Taylor, Rosalind Balcombe and John Nickalls (the publisher of this book) who played Percival Brown.

A choreographer was needed: who could do it? I knew at once – Donna Smith, the dancing school teacher, who instantly agreed to do it, even though she seemed to be dealing with many 'dancers' with two left feet and little co-ordination. It was hard work, for the cast and for us, being kept busy in the weeks running up to the performances at the High School hall in Wymondham.

On those nights the Mad 'Twenties came roaring in, with costumes, scenery changing, and players all highly acclaimed, as well as the music provided by the orchestra under the direction of Paul Donley. We had Tony Cleary on bass and David Pugh on drums with me on piano and Paul occasionally reverting to his clarinet.

It was a happy show, full of youthful zest with some memorable moments, including Royle's cheeky flirtation with Ros as Dulcie in 'It's Never Too Late', John and Nora reminiscing in 'Fancy Forgetting' and the boys and girls in bathing costumes 'Sur le Plage'. I enjoyed it all and recall how much pleasure it held for me – and still does.

This was the start of a happy relationship for me with the Ad Hoc entertainers who, from there went on to do more and more ambitious shows, continuing in June 1992 with *Guys and Dolls*, this time at Wymondham Central Hall. The show was directed and stage-managed by Nona Gray, a doyenne of theatrical fame, and produced by Wendy Nichols who herself played Miss Adelaide, dancer at 'The Hot Box', susceptible to colds in the head!

Nona wrote some programme notes,for the show which concluded: 'Some guys and dolls are more famous than somewhat, and this is true of two notable citizens, namely a very high flyer indeed called Sky Masterson and Miss Sarah Brown, the one hundred-percent-eyed doll from the Save-a-Soul Mission. You may wonder how these two became acquainted, seeing Sky is not in the business of saving souls and Miss Sarah not calling the shots at a crap game, but if you hang around this joint for long enough you will see things for what they are. So, sit down, take it easy no matter what, and furthermore enjoy the spectacle'.

There was a degree of panic which arose when, with a fortnight to go, two actors pulled out of the production and the rôles of Nicely Nicely Johnson and Benny Southstreet were taken over by Martin Spriggs and Martin Carruthers, both putting in splendid performances.

The musical director was again Paul Donley, having a seven-piece orchestra, with the jovial Don Brewer on drums, Jan Hytch on trumpet and John Matthews on sax. Into the lives of the Ad Hocs stepped Jimmy Skene on first violin who astounded the second violinist, Geraldine Evans, with his amazing virtuosity – on the violin that is. He had the time of his life, telling me how it took him back to his life as a pit musician playing for the Ivor Novello shows in London.

For me, it all went well on the Thursday, the first night, but on the second gremlins were at work when a sheet of music brushed away one of my contact lenses, leaving me only half-seeing the dots, giving me a difficult and uncomfortable time.

Since you can hardly go scrambling around in the middle of a show looking for a dropped lens, you have to wait until afterwards otherwise the audience might misconstrue such activity as part of the action. Needless to say it was never found and I had to use my second pair for the last night, the climax of a highly successful production with the proceeds going to the 'refurbishment of Central Hall'.

The gremlins were round again on the second night. However not with me personally this time, but with the show, for suddenly, half way through, all the lights failed. The stage lights, the spots, the house lights, all went off with, it seemed, little prospect of them being restored quickly for as I recall, Wymondham's electrician was on holiday.

What should we do? Give the audience back their money, give them a chance to come another night, or what? As there seemed a slight hope that somebody would be able to put some wires together to lighten our darkness (for indeed it was growing dark by then) we decided to give the audience some impromptu jazz, known in certain musical quarters as a 'jam session'. Wonder of wonders, it worked with the crowd showing their appreciation and actually roaring for more, as the jazz standards poured forth, with Jimmy and Paul delighting the people who looked upon it as a bonus and thought we should be paid accordingly. Eventually light was restored and the show went on with no further gremlin interference, but I know that many people had enjoyed that unexpected jazz interlude.

In 1993, following a successful show entitled *Seventy Years of Broadway*, a compilation of American show hits, the Ad Hocs put on Irving Berlin's *Call Me Madam* at Central Hall in June.

The numbers, all typical of Mr Berlin's genius, were sung well, the audience particularly enjoying the famous duet 'You're Just in Love'. We had an orchestral line-up under Paul Donley's baton, this time with Sylvia Watering on second violin, Geraldine Evans playing flute and clarinet and Andrew Dyson on alto sax and clarinet.

Again, Nona Gray directed while Wendy Nichols produced, and *Call Me Madam* was fairly successful, despite not having capacity audiences. I know the cast and the musicians enjoyed themselves which was important and must have showed. I suppose my own best recollections are of a fine performance by June Harrison as Sally Adams with those of Oz, Wendy, Royle, Ros and Nora in good support, plus a variety of curious American accents.

Finding a musical suitable for a small company isn't easy, particularly when you need to attract a paying public, which is why there followed a few years for the Ad Hocs with home-spun shows, the first in May 1994 entitled *Around the World in Eighty Minutes*. As the title suggests, it was a miscellany of songs and dances from around the globe with colourful costumed scenes, Wendy Nichols producing, directing and choreographing it all.

Into the musical frame came my old friend Joe Dade, who for the French set came on stage in beret, striped T-shirt and neckerchief to play his musette accordion, looking and sounding every bit 'l'accordionist de Paris'.

Jimmy Skene's rôle was something to remember. My friend Jean Swain had brought him a head-scarf from Egypt and Wendy fitted him up with the most absurd ear-rings, presenting him as a Hungarian gipsy violinist. In this guise he played Monti's 'Czardas' at a furious rate, looking totally bizarre, though never losing his professional composure, save after the very last note, leaping (yes, at 80) with the cry 'Hi!'.

The show was so popular with folk unable to get seats that Wendy put it on again in the October with equal success.

Fifty years after the ending of hostilities in Europe, the Ad Hocs, like so many other groups of entertainers decided to put on a show to commemorate 1945. In May, *Bless 'Em All* was staged with a plethora of wartime songs, cameos and uniforms evoking an era to bring memories flooding back to many of the audience and creating an historic atmosphere for those too young to remember.

With so many American ex-servicemen over in Norfolk for the commemorative events, it was no surprise to find some of them in our audience with emotions spilling over.

Included in the orchestra I had the brilliant Ivan Tooes on saxes and clarinet, who although he doesn't read a note of music, can play any tune, and also Joe Dade with his accordion. We needed a trumpet player for both the 'Forties sound and the Glenn Miller effects but getting the right person was a problem until I remembered that Jimmy Skene had been playing trumpet for most of his musical life. Could I persuade him and if so, how could we (he) overcome the false teeth problem, the very reason he had forsaken the trumpet in the first place?

In his very matter of fact way Jimmy said: "I'll do it."

I said, "Are you sure?"

"Yes; can you get me a trumpet, Tony?"

My ex-teaching colleague Rod Kibble had a trumpet which was not being used, so without further ado I asked Rod if Jimmy could borrow it and he agreed at once.

With two months to go to *Bless 'Em All* Jimmy now had his trumpet, fully resolved to be playing certain numbers on it on the three nights.

Now there are a number of things I don't know about our trumpet player's rejuvenation. Firstly, I'm not certain who suggested to Jimmy that he fix in his dentures with glue, nor secondly what brand he used, but I do know that he did. Thirdly, I have no knowledge of any comments or remarks made by the good people of Eaton as he practised for those two months, religiously every day, sometimes twice in the same day. Jimmy's window-cleaner assured me how good the sound was and how much he enjoyed listening, but I can't be certain just how many shared his enthusiasm.

As for the music in the show itself. I thought it was brilliant with Ivan's powerful lead on sax or clarinet and wonder boy Skene playing his trumpet faultlessly each night, especially in the difficult 'In the Mood'.

There was high praise from the Americans too, whom we met a couple of days later in a repeat of part of the show at Great Ellingham, near to where they had been based during the war and where the Ad Hoc players Robin and Ann Nash live.

Those wartime commemoration concerts were extremely emotional, the recollections of those horrendous times stirring many thoughts and I saw many a tear-stained face each night. Of course, like the other musicians I knew all the numbers which I suppose dates us, though I have never ceased to marvel at the beautiful words and music that came from such a tragic period in the history of mankind.

Ian (Oz) Topliff had married Wendy Nichols earlier in the year when Jimmy Skene and I had played at the blessing service and also at the reception at Little Melton Village Hall, augmenting with Ivan Tooes on sax and clarinet and Joe Jenkins on drums.

In October 1995, the Ad Hocs ventured into the world of Olde Tyme Music

Hall with much success, the 'chair' being shared by Royle Drew and Peter Wilson, one of them in each half. 'Outstanding' performance in that particular show was Wendy (now Topliff) singing 'Waiting at the Church' – outstanding, due to her 'bump' which was to become son George.

The other surprise for the audience that night was the appearance of Royle as the 'Galloping Major', not that he wasn't in the programme and listed as such but that he pranced on to the stage minus his trousers which, since it hadn't been expected, caused considerable laughter which tended to obscure what the song was about, although no one seemed to care, least of all Royle.

There are a number of questions I asked myself with regard to that cameo. Did he do it deliberately, or was he simply too rushed in a change-over? Was he aware of his condition either before, or when he was on stage? Or had he been bribed? Well, I did hear rumours to the effect that he might be 'persuaded' to repeat the performance, but of this and other conjectures I shall never be sure. Suffice to say it became a talking point for much of Wymondham and district long after.

In June 1996, the Ad Hocs put on a show called *Rags to Riches* at Hethersett New Hall, following it with another Music Hall in November entitled *Chiefly Yourselves* with Martin Spriggs as chairman.

A concert of *Ad Hoc Favourites* in June 1997 was followed by *Your Own, Your Very Own* in October and November, with Martin Spriggs again chairman, having a 'spot' of his own with the first and second of Stanley Holloway's 'Albert' trilogy. I think most of the audiences these days know 'There's a famous seaside place called Blackpool that's noted for fresh air and fun' with all the verses but the return of Albert is less well-known and still causes much laughter, just as it did with Martin.

An Evening of Romance was performed in May 1998 at Hethersett, being a concert packed with love songs, from the overture music from *Love Story* to beautiful numbers such as 'You'll Never Know', 'Night and Day', 'The Way You Look Tonight' and 'Love is Here to Stay' to the final song 'Love Walked In'. The theme was charming, we all loved the numbers and the audience did too.

What I remember most about that evening was poor Ivan Tooes feeling so ill and struggling to play, which led him to absenting himself for the second night. A prolonged illness followed, involving a thyroid condition, thrush and an onset of diabetes with Ivan declaring when I visited; "Tony, this is the end. I shall never play again".

Happily, it never turned out that way, for the medical people sorted out his various problems which was a good thing, since Ivan had a bookful of gigs to fulfill.

In November of that year the Ad Hocs returned to their good old stand-by,

Above: *David Perkins*.

Previous page: *Joe Dade in the St Stephen's underpass.*

Above: *Peter Fenn during his
days at Anglia Television.*

Left: *David Valentine.*

Above: *Jimmy Beaumont.*

Right: *Ivan Tooes.*

Facing page: *Colleen and Colin Harris.*

Above: *Barry Bryant.*

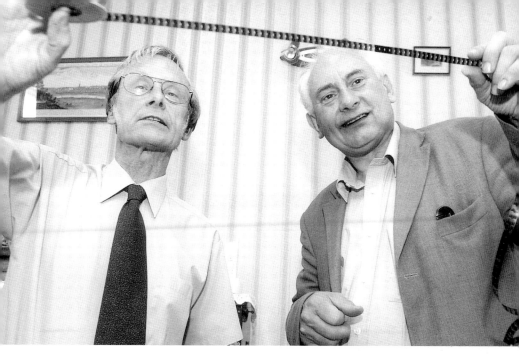

Above: *David Cleveland on the right, with Alan Cleaver.*

Below: *The Orchestra in rehearsal for* Wizard of Oz.

Above: *Ad Hoc's production of* The Boy Friend.

Below: *The original 'Tony and Friends'.*

the Music Hall, this time entitled *A Little of What You Fancy*, a song from the repertoire of Marie Lloyd. To create atmosphere for the audience we had Edward Murray-Harvey with his barrel organ play before the show and during the interval.

Included in the programme was a very funny Edwardian melodrama with many familiar ingredients such as the simple couple in their cottage and the unscrupulous landlord, played by Royle who really wasn't unpleasant enough which I suppose added to the fun. The funniest bit of it all was the Oscar-winning performance of Ros Balcombe as the unchaste daughter of the very simple but upright couple, who imbibed a quantity of alcoholic beverage believing it to be cordial. Her comical perambulations under the influence, even as dialogue was going on, were a sight to behold.

In the Olde Tyme Music Halls and the other shows, Wendy had sought to include young people and school children, and in 1999 the Ad Hocs reverted to the musicals to put on a production of *The Wizard of Oz* with Wendy's daughter Amanda in the lead as Dorothy. Son George was among a vast number of Munchkins, Royle played the cowardly lion, Robin the Tin Man and Oz made a superb Scarecrow, while Ros and Wendy were witches.

Since the large orchestra suggested by the theatrical agency would have taken up too much room and all the profits too, we had to think in terms of a 'small combo'. I asked Barry Bryant to play second keyboard, particularly as he had done the show before, so that between us we could produce some good sounds and effects and with John Winsworth on bass, Ivan Tooes on sax and clarinet and Joe Jenkins on drums, it all gelled very well.

Scenery, costumes and stage effects were splendid and recalling W C Fields' advice of "Never work with animals and children", the youngsters proved their worth while we performed the version that did not include Toto, thus mercifully spared the animal bit.

In May 2000 there was yet another visit to the Olde Tyme with the exhortation *Let's All Go To The Music Hall* with the chairman David Hill contributing with 'Trees', affectionately known to musicians as the Dog Song. Included again was another Edwardian melodrama with a dashing military hero and a villainous Chinese crook. It was quite hilarious, particularly where Royle as the girl's father would enter in a shower of snow, despite it being June.

In the autumn came another ambitious enterprise with *The King and I*, the Rodgers and Hammerstein Siamese extravaganza with Oz Topliff shaving his head to give a fine performance as the King. Again the costumes, designed and made by Wendy were sumptuous, as were the sets and various effects.

I had Barry on second keyboard again, he having done the show at Coltishall air-base, Ivan again on sax and clarinet, the ever-dependable John on bass and this time Alan Brady on drums, a splendid reading percussionist, deputizing for Joe Jenkins.

It is a beautiful musical, albeit difficult, but the Ad Hocs came through well, receiving good acclaim. An ex-education colleague, John Burdett kindly loaned two gongs which gave an almost J Arthur Rank authenticity to the production which was certainly full of eastern promise.

In 2001, after a great deal of deliberating, the Ad Hocs put on *Oliver!* with a huge cast of workhouse children (in the play I mean), Wendy producing, directing, choreographing, doing costumes and just about everything. She played Nancy, Oz gave us a superb Fagin, Royle was Mr Bumble, Stephen Bussey was Sykes and the two young boy leads, Oliver and the Artful Dodger, were excellently portrayed by Joe Lankowsky and Tim Richardson.

My orchestral line-up was almost the same as before, except that Matt Clark played bass in place of John Winsworth. It's not an easy score but it was good fun and we all enjoyed ourselves immensely. Sykes actually had Bullseye the dog, but he accomplished the show without mishap (Bullseye, that is).

The show got its deserved plaudits for I think it was probably the best the Ad Hocs had done. I do have a particularly soft spot for the composer, Lionel Bart, who couldn't read music, couldn't write it and couldn't play it, but with help wrote a brilliant score straight from his heart, the words and music giving us all the atmosphere of the Dickens'story. I loved the Jewish influence present in some of the music, such as 'Pick a Pocket' and 'Reviewing the Situation', Bart himself, of course, being a Jew. We have the same kind of Hebrew sounds in Jerry Bock's *Fiddler on the Roof.*

The Ad Hoc entertainers strayed from home now and then to sheltered homes or retirement centres to give shows to 'Senior Citizens' usually from the Olde Tyme Music Hall repertoire or to Women's Institutes where the gallant band were always well-received. I was their orchestra, though in the years up to 1997 was augmented by Jimmy Skene, putting his all into violin gymnastics. What can I say about the Ad Hocs?

Sometimes in rehearsals I have wondered what the finished show would be like, always having in mind the old theatre cliché 'It'll be all right on the night' with a few doubts about its veracity.

However, in every case it has been all right on the night and in any case, those niggling doubts prior to opening must have been present in thousands of productions the world over. Just think of Mr Porter's lines in *Kiss Me Kate*: "Three weeks and it couldn't be worse... One week will it ever be right? Then out of the hat it's that big first night".

And everyone pours their heart and soul into it, they and thousands like them, just like the Ad Hocs.

Given their enthusiasm and zest with the dynamic and imaginative Wendy Topliff at the helm, they could go on for ever and certainly, assuming my fingers and other bits can manage it, I'd go with them. The only slight worrying drawback is the material, the choice of musicals on offer since I can't envisage a helicopter descending into Hethersett Village Hall, required in *Miss Saigon*, nor the roller-skating antics of *Starlight Express* and the massive effects of *Phantom of the Opera* would be out of the question.

Modern musicals are not really musicals in the true sense but staged extravaganzas with music added which could never be performed in the provincial theatres and never in a thousand years in the average village hall.

The theatre-going public that knew the musicals of yesteryear are no more with the patrons these days expecting bigger productions, losing sight of the wonderful music of shows now forgotten and gathering dust on theatrical agencies' shelves. Lloyd-Webber and Schoenberg have collared it all, well almost, with Noel Coward and Ivor Novello old hat. Richard Rodgers, Frank Loesser, Sandy Wilson, Julian Slade... who?

Last St David's Day when I played a selection of Ivor Novello's work, a lady came up to me and said: 'You know, I'd forgotten all about Ivor Novello."

I felt glad that she had recognized his songs, but saddened by what she said.

Andrew Lloyd-Webber has said we must keep the musical theatre alive to which I would add: "Hear hear", but let's encourage new writers of real musicals to produce shows for the hundreds of companies like the Ad Hocs to put on in village halls all over Britain. Otherwise, there'll be so many repeats of *Oliver!* and *The Boy Friend* and so on that the entire audience will know all the words off by heart.

Thank you Ad Hocs for your lovely shows, every one of which has given me so much pleasure as accompanist and figure so highly in my world of musical experience.

CHAPTER EIGHT

Sing
As We go

S HORTLY after my return from Canada in 1987 following the tragic death
of my wife Jane, David Perkins telephoned: "Tony, I've got to sing some
solos at Cromwell House in October. Would you be able to accompany me?"

Well, of course I would. I'd known David for a long time and played for
him at a number of functions over the years so I was used to his style and the
kind of songs he favoured.

On the evening in question David arrived at Greenways in dinner jacket
and Mercedes to set off for Cromwell House on Cecil Road in Norwich. On
the way there he told me that he was the star-billing wedged somewhere
between the songs of the Taverham Singers. Did I know them? No, not
personally, but I had heard of them, for their fame had spread beyond
Taverham to all points including Eaton. As we parked at Cromwell House, a
blonde lady of slight build in evening dress came out to meet us.

"Tony, this is Miriam Batterbee, conductor of the Taverham Singers." We
shook hands but Miriam was clearly agitated by something.

"David, our pianist has been taken ill. Do you think Tony could accompany
the choir, as well as play for you?"

Never one to let a fair damsel in distress continue so for long, I agreed at
once. Well, not quite at once, since I did think it might be a good idea if I had
a look at the music first, since there might just be too many notes for me to
cope with. After a brief scan through the music and margin notes from
Miriam, I sat myself at a dark-brown upright of around '7 out of 10' in my
estimation, playing the first half for the choir and with David's solos wedged
in between.

In the tea and biscuits interval the choir appeared to go into what I can only
describe as a huddle, such as you would see American football players do for
a game plan. Perhaps, I thought, it is strike plans for improved pay or maybe
some kind of choral ritual they have, which in any case is nothing to do with

me. As it turned out, it had everything to do with me for, very soon, Miriam came to me to ask if I would consider becoming permanent pianist to the choir, since it was the wish of them all. She asked if I would give them an answer at the end of the evening and, after the concert finished with a lovely version of 'Sunrise, Sunset' from *Fiddler on the Roof*, I told the Taverham Singers I would be pleased to become their regular pianist.

As they surrounded me their pleasure was obvious as Miriam said: "Meet Eve, Dot, Margaret, Paddy, Irene... .and this is another Margaret, Joyce, Gladys, Audrey, Rosemary, Thelma, Carolyn.. and another Margaret!"

"And I'm Frank," said one of the men, "and this is Bill and Leslie and Charles and Herbert."

"And I'm John Unsworth," said the bearded one, "and I've met you at Rex Hancy's; you're a teacher!"

"Indeed I am – like you," I replied, wondering how I would remember all those names.

It was a most pleasant end to an evening which had, in fact, opened up a new beginning for me to play with the renowned Taverham Singers.

It appeared that the Singers had lost their founder and conductor, Phil Richardson, when he had collapsed and died at a concert in Costessey and were now being led by Miriam Batterbee, the deputy conductor and a member of the sopranos.

When we met again at choir practice at the Methodist Church in Drayton, she asked me if I knew of anyone who would like to become the new conductor, something I promised I would think about seriously.

As I sat at the large and powerful light-coloured upright, which I must say was quite a good piano with a bright tone, I thought: "I know who would jump at the chance of fronting the choir – Paul Donley. He had been the conductor of a choir in his home town of Northampton, which by all accounts had been excellent (the choir – not Northampton). He'd be the very man".

I related this to Miriam who in turn told the committee which led to the ritualistic huddle and thence back to me with the go-ahead to ask Paul to consider the suggestion. Paul was clearly delighted at the prospect, suggesting that before any decisions were made, it would be best for him to look the choir over, preferably in concert and then, if he liked what he saw and heard, he would accept the position.

In fairness, that approach would also have to apply to the choir to look Paul over to see if they liked him.

With all this in mind, a concert was arranged for December at the Methodist Church, Drayton, to which Paul was invited, with refreshments afterwards when there would be a chance to meet the new man with the baton and sound out potential compatibility.

Of course, I'd worked with Paul once or twice, albeit in the jazz field, so we knew each other's capabilities.

At the social after the concert there was much talk, but following a brief meeting with the committee, Paul Donley became the new conductor of the Taverham Singers, leaving Miriam relieved (literally) and everyone seemingly delighted.

In the new year, the Wednesday practices were resumed, Paul at the helm with intimations that there would be a change of emphasis in the music with more variety in the programmes and surprise, surprise, a touch of swing or jazz. Whether or not anyone felt any antipathy I can't say but there was certainly a 'lift' about the style as practices got under way.

The singers did many concerts, some on 'home' ground while others ventured further afield, occasionally in Norwich itself, such as at Paul's church, the United Reform on Ipswich Road. Paul had a Korg keyboard which we used when pianos were either in a sad state or totally non-existent and I remember hiking it up a long staircase to one particular home for the elderly.

Sometimes the choir would be sharing the bill with another group such as the Taverham Band or the South Norfolk Symphonic Wind Band under director Mike Booty, who made a very fine sound (the band, not Mike). One of the most memorable of these was at Diss Corn Exchange for a superb Christmas concert to a packed hall of people who gave huge applause to both the band and choir.

The other one which sticks in my mind was when the two joined forces for a *Last Night of the Proms* at Saint Andrew's Hall in Norwich with a finale of massed flag waving to 'Land of Hope and Glory'.

Each year, Paul would enter the choir for the *Sing for Pleasure* concert at Saint Andrew's Hall which featured as many as a dozen choirs or more with the large number of participants more often than not outnumbering the audience.

These productions came in three phases: on the Saturday morning; each choir would attend for audition, the actual concert would be from seven in the evening, followed by a party with 'in-house' entertainment from various factions.

It has to be said it was a very long and often tiring day, which would require two trips into Norwich for the morning and evening or else staying in all day which would be even more tiring and quite expensive, with the cost of lunch and parking being uppermost.

The audition part was where each choir assembled on the stage of Blackfriars' Hall to sing three or four songs to a small panel of highly musically-endowed people, who, in the customary way of examiners, would sit writing copious notes during the performance, at the same time as selecting two from each choir's repertoire for the evening concert.

Sometimes, leaving the panel deliberating, choirs would go off somewhere in the city to give an informal recital to transient shoppers, inside or outside depending on the weather. I well remember one such performance by the Taverham Singers in front of the Assembly House attracting a large crowd who were most appreciative, some promising to come to the evening concert.

On return to Blackfriars' Hall everyone would hear the adjudication comments and learn which songs would be required for the concert and the order in which choirs or groups would appear.

As to the concert itself; it was full of colour and variety with some choirs and groups coming from other counties and, in one case, another country – Canada. The finale was invariably a commissioned choral work written by a highly-skilled musician, sung by the whole assembly and conducted by the composer. It has to be said that it generally turned out right, despite the fact that when choirs first received their copies there were some grave doubts about the work or the ability to cope with it.

There were years when those on stage for the finale outnumbered the audience, on more than one occasion due to the fact that the *Sing For Pleasure* concert clashed with the Lord Mayor's procession, which can only be put down to bad organization.

For my part, I enjoyed the concerts since I had the chance to play the great Bosendorfer grand for the Taverham Singers, as well as seeing and hearing so many good performances by visiting choirs, groups and musicians, many of whom we came to know at the party social afterwards in Blackfriars' Hall.

When supper was over, each participating group did a 'turn', some very amusing and others showing great versatility and musical skill. Paul and I added our contribution of the jazz spot with a few lively numbers which seemed to be appreciated. A chorus of Auld Lang Syne ended a happy evening with echoes of "See you next year" from everyone as they made their way out into the summer night.

I suppose the most memorable and emotional engagement for the Taverham Singers was that at Topcroft when the USAAF men came to commemorate the end of World War Two with a service at the church, followed by a concert and lunch at a nearby farm on the site of the old airfield. The tears flowed freely at the church and again at the farm when the singers gave a short concert in the barn surrounded by tractors and other bits of farm machinery.

I remember walking down the old runway with Paul, some members of the choir and a few United States' men. You could almost hear the B47s coming in, it was so atmospheric. Then it was back to the old mess huts, now carefully restored, for a magnificent spread, to listen to so many tales of the wartime experiences.

One other engagement I will relate: Paul knew a colourful gentleman called Inigo Monk, who was estate manager for Holkham Hall, and through that association, the choir came to sing at a charity concert in the private church in the grounds of Holkham. It was a magical night with the sun streaming in through the latticed windows as the choir sang so beautifully to a capacity audience (or should that be congregation?) with the ghosts of so many long-departed Holkham citizens looking on.

After the concert some of the hierarchy of the choir were asked back to the Hall for a delicious supper, presided over by Lord and Lady Coke, with other important guests sharing the gathering.

There stood a grand piano which Lady Coke invited me to play, an invitation I could scarcely refuse and together with Paul on his clarinet we gave the family and guests an impromptu concert which seemed to go down well.

I spent eight very happy years with the Taverham Singers, playing for their practice nights and many, many concerts, getting to know many of them and sharing some of their problems. After each concert the lovely lady called Paddy Carr would give Paul and me a bottle of sherry, taking great delight in doing so.

Nothing much changed, save that the great piano at Drayton Methodist church seemed to ail a bit, eventually being replaced by an electronic instrument (dear, dear). Singers came and went, an inevitable part of any institution, but Paul was there with the choir going, as they say, from strength to strength.

The Taverham Singers were very much a part of my musical life and I had the greatest pleasure in sharing their experiences for those delightful years with Paul Donley conducting.

One evening I happened to see a paragraph in Derek James' column in the *Eastern Evening News* where the Cringleford Singers were losing their pianist and were appealing for anyone to come forward to play for them. The footnote asked any interested musicians to contact Margaret Smith at her home.

I mentioned it to my father who wondered if I might not be taking on too much, whilst my daughter Elisabeth shared his opinion, though shall we say in more emphatic fashion.

However, as one who is so often told that I open my mouth to say "No" and out comes "Yes" and, as I have mentioned elsewhere, one who can never ignore a lady in trouble, I telephoned Margaret who duly arranged for me to visit her home in Cantley Lane, Cringleford.

She was a sparkly lady, brimming over with enthusiasm, clearly musically gifted and full of her choir and their achievements. Two surprises emerged at once: the first was that the Cringleford Singers were all ladies and the second was that their assistant accompanist was dear Joe Dade on the accordion who had not featured for some time in my musical world.

That I knew Joe was a great delight to Margaret, who was obviously formulating future plans even as we talked. Of course, I played her piano, if only to reassure her that I could manage more than 'Chopsticks' with one finger and we spent an enjoyable evening going through songs, some from her collection and others from the choir's repertoire.

Practices were held at a big house off Colney Lane which was the home of one of the choir called Helga, whose piano was of the large upright grand variety. It was a fine instrument, apart from the fact that it could not be pulled up to concert pitch which was probably due to a history of neglect. It meant, of course, that when Joe attended any practice we could not play together since we would be a semi-tone out with each other, which would make music lovers wince.

We had a few engagements at various old folks' places but it wasn't long before I introduced Margaret to Jimmy Skene whom she found highly talented and most amusing. She featured songs like 'Scotland the Brave' and 'Coming Through the Rye' especially for him I think, as well as giving him a solo spot in the concerts. I believe the ladies of the choir loved Jimmy immensely, looking upon him as a kind of musical mascot, something in which he wallowed with delight. He found a wonderful rapport with Joe who was often astounded at Jimmy's versatility, just as I was.

There were some outstanding concerts, such as the open air summer fixture held in Helga's garden at Cringleford, where a large crowd of local people would gather to sit on garden chairs listening to midsummer melodies, occasionally interrupted by the familiar showers of summer.

Generally, the second half of the concert would be continued in Helga's swimming pool (not actually in it, but around the outside), Joe, Jimmy and I perched precariously close to the edge with a considerable extension lead for Margaret's electronic keyboard at which I sat with an uncomfortably close view of the water. The choir would be at the other end of the pool which gave a few seconds' difference to their voices accompanying us musicians.

Afterwards there was a splendid buffet of sandwiches, cakes and tea, a few speeches of thanks with everyone declaring what a lovely evening they'd had.

The most eventful and memorable time with the Cringleford Singers was at Christmas when euphoria abounded and performances reflected the joy and spirit of the festive season. That may sound flowery but it was so, for Margaret and her ladies could flavour Christmastide with their own brand of magic.

Margaret Smith was undaunted by large crowds in big places for, minus any amplification, she would woo the hotel guests at the Post House, Ipswich Road, persuading them to do silly things as well as, of course, sing.

It was the same at the Norwich Arts' Club at Plumstead Road where Margaret made herself heard above the din from the bowlers and the bar to invite people to join in carols as well as listen to the set choir pieces with an occasional solo from her, sometimes unaccompanied.

In return there would be glasses of sherry, Jimmy's favourite sausages on sticks and the inevitable mountain of mince pies. I think Joe, Jimmy and I arrived at Christmas looking like mince pies, as well as becoming experts in the matter of taste.

For three and a half years I enjoyed the music and fun with the Cringleford Ladies' Choir who had such a wide variety of songs from classic to jazz and a medley I particularly recall of 'Songs of the Twenties'. They gave so many people a great deal of pleasure with Margaret always drawing her audience into the programme, ever encouraging their participation.

Madge Mildinhall, a Londoner, who had made her home in Taverham, ran a choir of retired folk calling themselves 'The Taverham Singing Seniors', a title that often became confused with Paul Donley's Taverham Singers.

Madge was a delightful lady who would plan a number of concert programmes which would be rehearsed at Taverham Village every Tuesday morning following a cup of coffee and a chat.

Having Tuesday mornings free for the most part, I would play for the Singers, later taking Jimmy Skene along for the ride as well as giving him a chance to join in playing the lovely selections of songs that Madge had put together. Many of them came from the 'Thirties which has to be the finest decade of songwriting with the 'Forties and 'Fifties added, with just occasionally a rarity thrown in.

Madge liked to use the verses of the songs, so sadly neglected by so many vocalists and bands and in present day writing non-existent. She would intersperse the choral numbers with solos from choir members like Frances Streten who sang 'Moon River', Joe Hoffmann gave us 'My Prayer', his brother Don 'Young at Heart' while Mario rendered 'Come Back to Sorrento'.

During practice sessions Jimmy would have a whale of a time doing amazing gymnastics on his violin particularly on the up-tempo numbers ending with exaggerated flourishes amid helpless laughter which I hear to this day.

There were sprinklings of concerts with the Singing Seniors at places like John Gale Court at Thorpe Marriott and the United Reform Church at Unthank Road where the piano was so flat it would have made Vera Lynn sound like Paul Robeson.

There was the thrill of a recording on local radio which included interviews with Madge, Jimmy and me when BBC Radio Norfolk visited Ethel Tipple Court at Hellesdon. I think the reporter had some difficulty in understanding the Aberdonian lingo from Jimmy Skene as well as finding him somewhat unbelievable. The background noises both during the singing and the interviews must have caused some frustration to the BBC engineers though I doubt if there were many calls of protest on the night.

Madge Mildinhall, apparently calm and cool, always 'fronted' the choir, announcing the songs in turn with an occasional funny story or joke thrown in. Much of the charm of this was that invariably she would either leave out a crucial point in the story or get the punch line wrong altogether, all highly amusing to the choir and us musicians. Near the end of a joke she would say: "Oh, I forgot to tell you..." whereupon the choir would dissolve into laughter as poor Madge realised the point of the tale was lost.

Two years running, the Seniors sang at Christmas at Somerfields' Supermarket at Catton where the staff all dressed up in costumes from children's stories and nursery rhymes. We were surrounded by Snow White, Alice, Robin Hood, fairies and gnomes as well as the inevitable Father Christmas who turned out to be Mike Alden of Spixworth Players, complete with grotto, sack and "Ho, ho, ho". After the choir had regaled the shoppers, with 'Ding Dong Merrily, 'Silent Night' and 'White Christmas' among others, there was orange drink or coffee and yes – you've guessed it – mince pies for everyone. A couple of posed photographs of the singers and me rounded off the afternoon's entertainment with a farewell "Ho, ho" from Santa and it was "Happy Christmas all" and off into the twilight.

Madge, like Margaret Smith, left an audience feeling happy and no doubt saying "I did enjoy that", and that's what entertainment is all about, after all.

One other choir I give mention to: 'Wings of Song', originated and led by Audrey Yates and with a fine pianist Rita Berchem, who after her retirement was succeeded by an equally-talented lady, Annette Jude.

I include Wings of Song, not because I sang with them (they were all female) but that I was guest artist for them on one occasion in 1997 at the Methodist Church, Hethersett. It was on that night that I presented my very first talk entitled *Norfolk As She is Spoke*, which I have to say went down extremely well and has done so ever since, something for which I may thank Audrey Yates, being her suggestion in the first place.

The talk itself is about Norfolk dialect, very much tongue-in-cheek, with some of my favourite Norfolk tales to round it off. It took off from that night with enquiries from all quarters asking me to give the same presentation. Nothing to do with music, unless it might be described as another 'string to my bow'.

With regard to the theme of this chapter, I call to mind snatches of sentences such as 'In quires and places where they sing..' which used to fascinate me as a boy as I thumbed my way through the prayer book instead of paying attention to a boring sermon.

Then there was that vocative and triumphant call from the psalmist: "Make a cheerful noise unto the Lord", encouraging a congregation to let forth their voices, regardless of any definition of harmony, a common enough feature of many wedding services, for example.

Choirs have to be trained, not only to sing together in harmony but in all the disciplines that go with it, so that a perfect performance results, in the same way that an orchestra would.

I well remember Cathy Restieaux' instructions to the children at Thorpe Hamlet school: "You train yourself not to move. The audience will soon notice anyone who scratches their nose!"

And: "If your mummy or your auntie waves to you on the stage, you take no notice, except you might frown at them."

Well, we've all seen it, haven't we? Even in adults: the Laurel and Hardy finger greeting, plus the silly grin. Dear Mrs Restieaux would have had a fit.

I've been lucky enough to have seen and heard some great choirs in my life, such as the Mormon Tabernacle Choir, King's College Cambridge Choir, the Red Army Choir, the Welsh National, the Luton Girls and smaller groups like the King's Singers, Les Swingles and the George Mitchell singers.

Some of the renditions were memorable for me, like 'Kalinka' from the Red Army, 'All Through the Night' from the Welsh which sends shivers down the spine, a piece of jazzed up Bach from the Swingles and George Mitchell's acapella version of 'Dem Bones, Dem Bones, Dem Dry Bones". Topping all of them would be Christmas carols from King's College which I can only describe as breathtakingly magic.

Perhaps I should have entitled this chapter with the Noel Gay song 'Let the People Sing' since this is just what choral work is: letting people join together in song for the enjoyment of others, hopefully not as was indicated on one church notice board with two announcements in juxta-position: 'Tonight's religious topic: What is Hell like?' With: 'Come and listen to the church choir'.

My time with the choirs I have written about was a great musical experience for me, together with a friendship and camaraderie that is special to those involved in the world of music, a world that knows no discord, only harmony.

CHAPTER NINE

Let Me
Entertain You

IN April 1991, I was invited to Sally Swain's twenty-fifth birthday party, not only as a guest but, as is generally my wont, to provide the musical bits. Sally was the only daughter of a great magician and friend Pat Swain (alias Harry Carson), and his wife Jean, who lived at Bracey Avenue in Sprowston and Sally, having recently become a member of the East Norfolk Operatic Society had invited members to her party.

Pat had no piano, probably for no other reason that he did not play one, or possibly the question of space, the bungalow having neither music room nor elastic walls.

My Casio keyboard fitted nicely into a corner as it so often did and for much of the evening I was playing 'music to suit all tastes', though I'm never quite sure if that is humanly possible. My good friend Jimmy Skene used to say: "If you try to please all of the people all of the time, you're half-way down the road to insanity!".

Two of the singers who that evening contributed to the entertainment were husband and wife Ernie and Vi Shaves, Ernie having been Sally's partner in an East Norfolk operatic production. During the interval, something that musicians enjoy, even though they sometimes have to find a corner of a kitchen to squat and balance a plate of buffet provender on one knee and a glass of something 'alcofrolic' (Pat's expression) on the other, I got chatting to Vi and Ernie, both 'foreigners' from London ,who told me that they had met and married in Dagenham in Essex where Ernie had worked for the Ford Motor Company.

He had cast an eye on Vi, a dancer in the Windsorettes troupe, and decided she was to be his sweetheart and, of course, eventually his bride. What better ingredients for such a union? He hailed from Bethnal Green (my maternal grandmother's home), she from Manor Park, and both loved music, singing and dancing.

They came to Norfolk in 1966 settling down in the village of Newton Flotman and fulfilling their musical dreams by singing in chorus parts of shows put on by the Norfolk and Norwich Operatic Society to include *White Horse Inn*, *Merry Widow* and *Sound of Music* in which Vi played a nun.

As well as this, they joined in the Gilbert and Sullivan romps put on by East Norfolk and Ernie also figured in the Martin Singers, a group of Norwich-based entertainers. I gathered from what they said that they also went out as a pair singing for old folks' clubs accompanied by their pianist Margaret Johnson whom I knew well from Eaton Rise. Margaret at that time was rehearsal pianist for East Norfolks and her husband Dennis, musical director.

Vi and Ernie told me that Margaret was unwell, unable to play for their next concert, and asked if I would agree to act as their accompanist at the Methodist Church hall in Rosebery Road in Norwich.

I agreed at once and met them on the appointed day, a bit early in order to have a look at the music just to make sure that it didn't have lots of difficult bits I couldn't manage. They asked me to do a 'piano spot' which turned out to be *Memories of Fred Astaire*, a selection of the numbers he danced to in those great films of the 'Thirties and 'Forties.

The little concert was a success, despite the tricky duet about 'Dear little donkey' having a difficult intro which didn't seem to have any bearing on the song that followed, and from that concert the three of us went on to do other engagements together.

That performance led me to think that I could take out, what used to be called, a 'concert party' to entertain not the troops but elderly people in homes and day centres. I remembered my Uncle Godfrey with his concert party *The Jolly Boys* who would provide songs, music and comedy to all and sundry in Norwich and district before the war and just after.

They included 'smoking concerts' which presumably meant singing and playing to folk in smoke-filled rooms, smoking being fashionable then, the public puffing away on pipes, cigars and cigarettes. How Uncle Godfrey et al managed to sing in such an atmosphere I don't know, although of course the dangers of smoking, including 'passive' smoking were not apparent in those days. I only have to have two or three people smoking near me when I am playing, to necessitate my hanging out my suit to air later, which leads me to believe that the time is not far off when smoking is banned in all public places, as indeed it is in Canada, and recently in Norway and Eire.

So it was that I gathered together quality entertainers to become 'Tony and Friends', a diversity for me during the day and some evenings as well.

There was Miriam Batterbee, she who had been the temporary conductor of the Taverham Singers and then returned to the front ranks of the sopranos after Paul Donley had taken over the baton. Miriam already knew Vi and Ernie from light-opera days with the Norfolk and Norwich Operatic, having been together in a number of shows. Now we were four...

Comedy was needed, so who better than Royle Drew from the Ad-Hocs, an ex-Norwich Union man who already knew Ernie Shaves, since Ernie had been in 'Supplies' in the same insurance company. Royle could give us – and the audience, Stanley Holloway monologues, some long-forgotten, to revive an aspect of entertainment from yesteryear. Now we were five...

Another musician? Could I persuade Jimmy Skene, the ex-pro, nearly eighty-years-young to come as soloist and also accompany me in opening selections?

Jimmy needed no persuading but leapt at the chance (as much as an eighty-year-old is able to leap), at once showing me his violin solos, complete with piano accompaniment which included Kreisler and Schubert with other favourites like 'Song of India', 'Standchen' and of course Monti's 'Czardas'.

Now we were six, and 'Tony and Friends' became a reality with the format of our concerts being the same construction at many venues: Jimmy and I would open with a selection from a show like *Oklahoma*, *Merry Widow* or *Showboat* or Jimmy's favourite *Memories of Ivor Novello* followed by solos and a duet from Vi and Ernie, after which Royle would regale the audience with a monologue like 'Albert and the Lion' (although this particular one had to be shelved after a while when we realised that the audience knew the words as well as he did – if not better!).

He was followed by Miriam giving us beautiful renderings of show songs such as 'Love is My Reason', 'If I Loved You' and her favourite introductory song from *The King and I* – 'Getting to Know You'.

After I had told a few Norfolk stories, everyone would get another turn with Jimmy's violin solo wedged in there somewhere until the finale heralded the end of an hour or so's show, generally received with resounding applause.

It became clear that we didn't have to advertise with engagements coming in a steady flow, I taking the bookings, Miriam acting as treasurer with everyone journeying separately to the venues, apart from Jimmy who came with me.

From the outset Jimmy kept a note book with the venues, the dates and what we played which ensured there was no repetition anywhere – one of the marks of his professional career.

It would be impossible to write an account of every place we visited, particularly where a concert passed without incident but, as all entertainers experience, there were things that happened worth recounting for the reader's enjoyment.

At Beeston Regis, Miriam couldn't be with us for a concert in the church where for the most part things went quite well, apart from the fact that the piano was raised up (I think on blocks) which gave the feeling of the pedal being poised in mid-air like a car accelerator.

The outstanding feature of that summer evening however, was a couple who sat at the back who never smiled or applauded all night. They looked so dead pan I wondered if they were cardboard cut-outs but in any case all of us found it very funny.

During Miriam's singing at the Crome Companions' Club at the Crome Community Centre, a gardener decided to cut the hedge with an electric trimmer right next to the hall windows. It did nothing for Miriam's solos and in fact was a pity since we had put on a cassette to record the afternoon's concert. The resultant recording does give the impression that Miriam and the gardener are in competition with one another.

At Cringleford Village Hall there was a tea set out where afterwards each of us was asked to sit next to a member of the club. Royle was asked to chat to a particular lady and inquired of her if she had enjoyed his part of the show, namely the monologues.

"You were very good," she replied, "except that I'm totally deaf and couldn't hear any of the words you were singing."

Of course, you can easily be put off if someone gets up and goes out in mid-performance, but when you've been some time in the business of entertaining, you get used to it. However, when two entire rows get up and leave, as happened during Royle's spot at the Dereham Road Baptist Church hall, he could be forgiven for thinking they were not too keen on him. It was explained afterwards that they were catching a 'bus to somewhere, maybe as Royle wickedly suggested: "A better class of show."

A mere couple of days later Royle was relating this incident to the good members of the Crome Companions (this time without hedge trimmer) who laughed heartily, picturing two rows of people walking out of his act. However, hardly had he begun his tale of 'Sam's Christmas Pudding' when the doors to the kitchens opened and in came two ladies with the tea trolleys, right on cue, which made everybody fall about laughing. Royle included.

I have to say that we had an excellent team with wide-ranging talent that blended so well together. The vocal items were provided by Vi and Ernie who would give a solo each, followed by a duet, one particular favourite being 'Sweethearts' by Victor Herbert and another 'The Keys of Your Heart' from *Maid of the Mountains*.

Ernie's solos included 'Girls Were Made to Love and Kiss', from Lehar's *Paganini*, and 'Song of Songs' which I recalled from my boyhood when my two uncles sang round the piano at 12 Buxton Road in Norwich.

Miriam's songs included those by Ivor Novello 'My Dearest Dear', 'My

Life Belongs to You' and the ever-popular 'We'll Gather Lilacs' which was sung by thousands as they lined the route at the composer's funeral. To these she added such numbers as 'I Was Never Kissed Before' (Vivian Ellis) and Gershwin's 'The Man I Love'.

Royle provided the comedy with monologues from the vast list by Marriott Edgar and Stanley Holloway including 'The Battle of Hastings', 'Magna Carta', 'Three Ha'pence a Foot' and the oldest of all – 'The Wedding'. Others were about Sam or Albert, including the latter's lesser-known adventure in which the young man returns from being eaten by the lion.

Later on, Royle introduced audiences to 'Nobody Loves a Fairy When She's Forty' appearing in tutu, tights and wig, complete with flexible wand to tell the sad vocal of how modern times had deprived the fairy of top spot in the popularity stakes.

Audiences' reactions would vary from sheer disbelief to semi-hysteria, from stifled chuckles to helpless, uncontrollable laughter.

On one occasion a dear little lady, after seeing the phenomenon followed by Royle's return in 'mufti' said to him:

"I guessed that was you all the time."

On many occasions, adoring females wanted to take him home, and on one other performance a gentleman from the audience expressed a similar desire. For my part I would add some Norfolk stories which seemed to go down well, with even 'foreigners' like Vi and Ernie enjoying the strange Norfolk humour. Each show would open with Jimmy and me playing a selection from a show and because of Jimmy's great ability to 'busk' anything, we did arrangements together with no music, what musicians call 'head arrangements'.

We presented show after show, some from Rodgers and Hammerstein or Jerome Kern, Cole Porter or Irving Berlin, although Jimmy loved the tribute to Ivor Novello the best while mine was the salute to Gershwin.

Completion of the musical content was in Jimmy's capable hands when he would choose a violin solo from his great collection which included Kreisler favourites such as Schoen Rosmarin or Liebeslied, Chanson d'Indou by Rimsky-Korsakov, Slavonic dances by Dvorak or, of course, Monti's Czardas. In the latter days of his career Jimmy worked hard on Sarasate's 'Zigeunerweissen', delighting many an audience with a dexterous interpretation of a difficult gipsy air.

Those shows were good, even though I say it myself for there was polish in the presentation as well as the variety which audiences sought and Jimmy, the ex-professional rated it very highly. The six of us were able to give a balanced performance of around an hour and a quarter, invariably leaving the people wanting more.

Of course, audiences would vary greatly with some none too well-behaved who, like children, would find things to talk about during a performance. I remember one such section at Douro Place when Ernie, normally a placid man, threatened to walk out if the talkative element didn't cease their chattering.

At the hall of St Mary's church, Silver Road, we experienced a heavy thunderstorm, where the rain beating down on the glass roof not only tended to drown out the singers but also caused the elderly folk to panic somewhat.

At Westwood House, by St Thomas's church on Earlham Road, they had a lift to take our gear to the upstair room where we were to entertain. I do believe that the lift manufacturer had been a highly temperamental individual who had left his personality with his construction, since the said lift door would suddenly close to leave one of us or some of our gear inside. After a few visits to the home we would get used to dashing from the lift to try to defeat its attempts to crush or trap individuals, though on one occasion I mis-timed things and received a vicious blow on my person. As I remember, one or two of the group took to using the stairs, preferring not to take any chances.

We entertained at some marvellous homes and to some delightful people, too many in number to mention them all. We had our favourite venues such as concerts we gave at the beautiful house of Ann Gotts at Mulbarton Common. Ann had been Ann Bridgeman at Thorpe Hamlet School as a pupil of mine, who had been in one of my operettas: 'Double Dutch'.

My re-acquaintance with Ann came about through Vi Shaves, and the elderly folk from around Mulbarton were invited to Ann's home for a concert and tea on a fairly regular basis. When we first went there, Ann's mother was part of the audience who loved the mix of song, music and humour, with the six of us gathered around Ann's piano, providing the sounds of yesteryear to an ageing group of people. Afterwards there would be a sumptuous tea set out on tables in Ann's conservatory with the sort of delights highly favoured by Jimmy – and me, of course.

We had highly receptive audiences at Chapel Field Road Methodist Church, Corton House, Doughty's Hospital, Jessopp Road Luncheon Club, Poringland Over Sixties, Rosebery Road and Salhouse Village Hall.

At the Cedars, off Albemarle Road, we met the doyenne of Norwich opera, Ivy Oxley, who was living there in retirement and seemed to delight in the reminiscences as well as giving high praise to our performances, particularly to Miriam who had been part of Mrs Oxley's operatic entourage.

Elsie Beales was a remarkable lady, living in the complex known as Foulger's Gap at Ber Street. Miriam Wilson, the warden asked us to entertain at Elsie's hundredth birthday when we saw the Queen's telegram, and I invited her (Elsie, not the Queen) to play the piano as part of our entertainment programme.

We had been there many times on the run-up to her hundredth but this, of course was a very special occasion, more especially since Elsie had just had her cataracts done.

"I can now read the music," she said triumphantly. "Up to now I've been playing it out of my head but now I don't even need glasses."

At Foulger's she played to the residents almost daily: anything from Chopin to Scott Joplin which was a delight to everyone and something she loved to do.

When we went there to entertain, I would always include Elsie in the programme, announcing her as a special guest-artiste mid-way through the concert.

"What shall I play?" was always her opening line.

"Anything you like," I would reply, whereupon Elsie sat herself at the piano to give us Sinding's Rustle of Spring or Beethoven's Fur Elise. Loud applause would follow, after which Elsie would launch into 'The Entertainer' by Scott Joplin, all the way through, repeats and all, with barely a fault. Not bad for a centenarian.

When, at 103 Elsie fell and broke her hip, everyone wondered if the wonderful lady had played her last show but not a bit of it. Within three weeks she was out of hospital minus frame or sticks, making tea for her visitors at her flat in Foulger's. All were astounded, not least of all her grandson Simon Cullum, my piano tuner.

When the local newspaper did an article about the remarkable Elsie, she castigated the reporter for having the affrontery to describe her piano playing as 'thumping'.

"I do not thump," she declared, "I PLAY the piano!"

Each year we went to help celebrate Elsie's birthday until she died aged 107 at Mill Croft where I understand she played to the residents every day at 10am. A great lady, a wonderful character, one whom I was privileged to know.

During this time of concert party work, as Tony and Friends, we relied entirely upon the pianos at the various venues. Those who have read my first book S'Wonderful will know that I have given pianos marks out of ten according to their condition, efficacy and general sound with marks deducted for tonal faults, pedal problems and other peculiarities. The reader might therefore care to share with me some of my experiences encountered with pianoforte eccentricities at various establishments on our perambulations around the county.

Naturally enough,there were some good ones, very good ones, such as the superb German upright at Dereham Road Baptist church hall. It is a giant black instrument with that wonderful power, especially in the bass that is so typical of German pianos and how I loved to play it.

I delighted in playing the beautiful grand at the Norwich Citadel in St Giles when we gave a concert to the old folk there one afternoon, and I met the most handsome full-size Yamaha grand at the church on the Norwich ring road opposite Heartsease School. At the time, the Gothic Club, retired workforce of Laurence and Scott, met there. The hall was very long indeed but the sound of that great instrument carried all the way down.

The three pianos I have just mentioned were in the ten out of ten category, cared for and maintained regularly, just as they ought to be. I can never understand why any piano, once somebody's pride and joy, lovingly played and looked after, should suddenly be reduced to a cacophonous heap with an outer case stained and blemished with marks, rings and cigarette stains. Inwardly I cry for them, for they don't deserve such treatment and those responsible should be horse-whipped. Most of the pianos we came across were in my rating around six or seven out of ten which means they were passable and playable, albeit some in need of a tuner. Into this category were the pianos at Jessopp Road, Laurel Court, Rosebery Road, Roxley Hall, Chapel Field Road, Cringleford and Foulger's, to all intents and purposes in good order – just.

At Hempnall Mill Hall they have a ship's piano, so small with around four octaves which tends to throw the pianist – literally off the top end.

How about those pianos that just didn't make it on the Tony Ireland scale?

Well, there was one at the United Reform Church hall at Unthank Road, neglected and sad, it had probably been subjected to fluctuating temperatures which set it permanently just over a tone flat which presented a problem for any tuner worth his salt, In tune with itself, but never able to achieve 'concert' pitch, it meant that sopranos became contraltos, tenors became baritones and instrumentalists just had to manage as best they could.

We had arranged a big concert at Drayton Village Hall, a charitable affair raising funds for Drayton Methodist Church and the Drayton surgery. In the cast were Norma Wick and Ron Sallis, as well as Miriam and Royle, plus guest pianist Ian Shepherd with yours truly accompanying.

Highlights of the performance were Royle and Norma with 'Doctor Doctor' (the Peter Sellers' classic) and Miriam and Ron singing the waltz duet from *Merry Widow*.

The village hall's notorious piano, stuck as ever well below concert pitch, was a headache nobody needed for a big concert, particularly when a fine pianist like Ian Shepherd was booked to play solos.

A few days before the concert I telephoned the lady who was 'custodian' of the village hall to request that my tuner, and piano doctor, Simon Cullum, be able to come and tune the said instrument. With her reply I was reminded of the old music hall song: 'You Can't Do That There 'Ere'.

"We have our own tuner," she said, "Tom (I think that was the name, though it could have been Horace) always sees after the piano and he doesn't allow anyone else to touch it."

I gathered that the afore-mentioned gentleman was a jack-of-all-trades who did a bit of this and that, probably sheared sheep or cut down forests and, just for good measure, tuned village hall pianos. It was patently clear that no other tuner would be allowed to touch the Drayton Village Hall piano on pain of death and I was assured that it had been tuned: "only last week".

So there it was, no one allowed to touch the piano which meant that we (Ian Shepherd and I) would have to take our chances.

Incidentally, some years later when I was playing for Madge Mildinhall's Singing Seniors at Drayton Village Hall using that very same piano I found that two of the keys were jammed solid like Siamese twins, refusing to play independently. I suspect somebody had broken the rules and tried to tune it without the knowledge of the official village piano doctor. It was either that or a frustrated pianist had wielded a sledge hammer and attempted to bludgeon the unfortunate instrument into submission.

What of the concert then? A great success, both musically and financially, with around £500 being raised for the two charitable causes. Despite the vagaries of the piano, Ian gave us some good solos and although the piano was well below concert pitch, Norma did not become Greta Garbo nor Royle Paul Robeson and Ron and Miriam accomplished their songs well, ending with a delightfully sung duet.

On a recent visit to the village hall I read a notice pinned to a cloth covering the piano which stated: 'On No Account is this Piano to be Moved'. I must say I was extremely tempted if only to see what might happen...

Was that the worst piano we had come across? Well, no – not quite.

Vi Shaves' mother spent her last years in Hanover Gardens (no, not in Germany) at Mulbarton, near Norwich, and we were asked to go there to entertain the residents in their communal room. The six of us duly met, at first in the wrong place (though this was not an unusual feature of our programme) and then at the retirement home.

In the long lounge stood an upright piano against a wall.

On opening the lid I ran my hands over the keys when a mixture of intuition and experience told me that it was 'down', something one could describe as an understatement. It was that down it made our singers strain on the lower notes while Jimmy's violin took on viola proportions if not 'cello' with the anxiety that his bridge might collapse through lack of support.

Added to all this was the fact that the loud pedal had one hell of a squeak and, although I joked to the audience about the piano's pet mouse, it did grow disconcerting as the evening went on, there being no 'lift' to our performance.

It was as a result of this last piano that I decided to buy a keyboard, since it was clear that many pianos at various venues were a liability, so much so that we could never rely on finding anything much better than a 'six out of ten'.

So it was then that I found myself in Jack White's shop in St Benedicts, in Norwich, surrounded by all manner of keyboards. Why Jack White's? I had read up about electronic pianos in a variety of magazines to find that 'Roland' came top of the authentic piano sound, one of the makes sold at Jack White's. Dave Sadler, the manager, knowing just what I was looking for, showed me a selection of keyboards, all like twentieth century humans having a number.

"What you need is the Roland FP1," said Dave.

"Do I?"

"As good as any grand."

I tried it out and had to agree. It was powerful, having as many notes as a grand with a resonant bass.

Dave went on: "It has weighted keys, is touch sensitive and this is the last one left."

What he meant was that the keys had the same action as any real piano, that hitting the keys softly gave a soft response or hit hard had a loud response.

It meant also that it was not a tinny, toy effort, but a mighty, heavy instrument, only portable to the extent of being mindful of a hernia, possibly a double. As to being the last one left, I assumed he meant in the shop, something with which we are all familiar. I jest: Dave is the most genuine of men and indeed I was to learn later that the FP1 went out of production soon after my visit to Jack White's.

Did I buy it? Why yes, of course, together with a strong sack barrow to transport it, for it was twice as heavy as it looked to be sure.

No longer did we need to worry about wrecks, or apologies of pianos, for 'Roland' went everywhere with us, giving all of us back the 'lift' we needed. Miriam, Vi and Ernie were able to sing at normal pitch, Jimmy didn't have to fiddle about with tuning pegs (forgive the pun) while I delighted in playing solos and demonstrating what Roland could do. By this I mean that not only could he produce a variety of sounds but when 'instructed' could perform with my aid (the demo tape within).

We were now seven, with Roland behind us, as it were, and 'Tony and Friends' grew in popularity with each concert to the delight of us all. Despite the warm acclaim, the dozens of newly-formed friendships, the camaraderie of the group and everyone's kindness, I knew something was missing.

Almost six years had passed since I lost Jane and I felt the loneliness that I know so many others like me have experienced, the void that becomes so apparent early in the morning and late at night and the sight of so many friends in their 'pairs'.

The words of the Gershwin song haunted my mind in the months that followed:

"There's a somebody I'm longing to see,
I hope that she turns out to be,
Someone who'll watch over me."

Someone who'll watch over me...

There's no such person I told myself; not a permanent relationship, as the expression goes.

I'd had a flirtation with Pat and Jean's 'adopted' daughter Annie, who lived in Portsmouth, and I'd enjoyed a lovely friendship with Cathy Soame-Hook who had been widowed for some time – but that was it.

Life can be full of surprises as I have found and early in 1994 I was planning the content of a programme with Miriam when I realised that she was that 'somebody' of my Gershwin song.

She was there – all the time and like me, was unhappy, since her marital life had soured.

It seemed that the words of the song applied to her too and a chemical reaction occurred which drew us together romantically.

My Gershwin composition now changed to another:

"Love walked right in and chased the shadows away...
One look and I forgot the gloom of the past,
One look and I had found my future at last...
When love walked in with you."

My life, it seemed, had begun again, although any thoughts I might have had about sailing calm waters would be rudely preceded by decidedly stormy conditions.

I don't intend to burden the reader with all the difficulties Miriam and I had to face up to over the next few months but, as in such cases, major problems had to be overcome, not least of all Miriam's divorce.

It was strangely coincidental that once we knew we could 'go public', we told the others in the group – Vi, Ernie, Royle and Jimmy at Cromwell House, the very place where I had first met Miriam seven years before. They were all pleased for us which was both a joy and a relief, for it goes without saying that not everybody shared that same pleasure.

In May 1995 we were married at Churchman House Registry Office in Norwich followed by a blessing service at St Andrew's church, Eaton. My brother David and his wife Cathy came over from Canada with David acting as my best man and both our daughters were there, among some 140 guests.

Music abounded at the ceremony with my organist friend David Morgan playing for the service as a wedding gift, his rendition of Widor's 'Toccata' at the end being magnificent. Naturally with all the musicians and choristers present, the singing was explosive.

Little Jimmy Skene, who had practised assiduously for weeks played 'Jesu Joy of Man's Desiring' and 'Meditation' by Massenet impeccably, and Phil Penn played 'Trumpet Tune' on his cornet.

An impromptu concert featured at the reception (where Barry Bryant played the piano beautifully – another wedding gift) with Jimmy Skene showing off his Stephane Grappelli skills.

Members of 'Wings of Song' led by Audrey Yates gave us 'Keep Young and Beautiful' and Miriam delighted everyone with the Kern-Hammerstein song 'All the Things You Are'.

All the musical friends, and others who were there, are too many to name, but it was a very happy occasion with the sun shining through the afternoon as folk spilled on to the lawns of Town Close Pre-Prep School. Usually at weddings the bride and groom are waved off by the guests who are left behind to fill the aftermath. With ours, we were the very last to leave and hasten off to Southwold for two days at 'The Swan Hotel'.

We splashed out for a Mediterranean honeymoon on SS *Canberra* (ugh, another pun) and on the voyage took part in the passengers' concert when Miriam sang 'I Could Have danced All Night' and I played a selection from *Me and My Girl*.

During this time Miriam was working as a secretary to the Archdeacon of Norwich from 9am until 4pm, commuting every day from our house in Eaton. This meant that she was only able to take part in evening concerts, leaving me to find artistes to join us for the daytime shift.

Her place was often filled by Margaret Gallant, who rendered some lovely solos, as did Elsa Perry and June Harrison. Margaret came more often than the other two and I would refer to her as 'my afternoon wife'.

Sometimes we would have Harry Heddon to give us his Scottish songs with a few anecdotes thrown in, told in his lovely Scottish brogue.

Later in 1995 Miriam and I made a momentous decision to move from Greenways, Eaton, into the countryside of Norfolk, having discovered a bungalow in the quiet little village of Kirstead, not far from Brooke.

On 6 January (Epiphany) 1996 we moved into our new home which we named 'Linden Lea' from the Vaughan Williams' song, even though there is not a linden tree in sight, but the apple tree 'do lean down low' there.

A pre-war song was entitled 'Our Bungalow-of Dreams' and this was it. At least, to us it was, though there were many who said: "Whatever do you want to live out in the styx for?"

Well, there were drawbacks of course, such as Miriam having to journey in to Norwich each day, contending with the rush-hour traffic around 8.15am, and again at 4.30pm. If ever there was a misnomer it was the 'rush hour', since 'rushing' was just about impossible.

The great thing about our rustication was the peace and quiet 'far from the madding crowd' and the hubbub of the city, a setting which was clearly ideal for calm thoughts in contemplation of my first book *S'Wonderful*.

As for Tony and Friends, the concerts went on, both afternoons and evenings, my having a 'day wife' and an 'evening wife' with the only snag of having to make a trip to Norwich to collect Jimmy Skene from Eaton. I didn't look upon it as a snag, however, since he was such a fine trouper and a delightful little man from whom I learned much. He had two short holidays with us at 'Linden Lea' which he described as Tony and Miriam's 'Music Academy and Health Farm'.

He and I would practise all sorts of solos and selections to use in future concerts, followed by supper when Miriam arrived home; Jimmy's favourites were sausage and mash and liver and bacon with his choice vegetable of butter beans.

Each concert we did saw all of us gaining in confidence, becoming more and more polished, all reflected in the warmth of the reception, the length of the final applause and the eagerness to re-book us.

After one such concert at St Peter's, Park Lane, Ernie, complaining of feeling unwell, paid a visit to his doctor who prescribed a higher dose of medication for the polymyalgia from which Ernie suffered.   This seemed to have an adverse effect which led to Ernie having hospital tests, the results of which were not good, cancer being diagnosed.

Ernie Shaves died in August 1996 leaving a grieving Vi and a sadness which our group felt deeply. We would miss his cheeky delivery of 'Girls Were Made to Love and Kiss', his dapper little steps in many of his lighter songs and his infectious chuckle we had grown to know and love.

Small wonder then that at his funeral service on 22 August a great number of people from the world of entertainment came to pay their last respects, for Ernie held great affection for so many singers and musicians.

Of course, concerts would never be quite the same again, particularly for Vi but, in the world of entertainment, the show must go on as they say and Ernie, I know would have endorsed that.

We would have 'guest' artistes join us from time to time, perhaps when one or another of us was unavailable for any reason. With Miriam at work during the day, I would ask both singers or musicians to come along with the occasional visit from Stan Ferrari with his monologues when Royle was away.

Stan, who had his own entertainment group, was quite different from

Royle, telling his tales in his distinctive London accent and I remember in particular 'The Hole in the Road' in which a road digger imagined his invitation into 'the big house' at Christmas. Other yarns were 'The Single Hair' which recounted how a balding man endeavoured to preserve his last remaining hair by having it stuffed, and another was the remarkable 'family tree' rhyme entitled 'She was only a miner's daughter'.

Audiences loved him, just as we did; sadly, he too has made his last exit.

Musicians who joined us were Jimmy Beaumont with his guitar, who seemed to hit it off well with Jimmy Skene, the former strumming a Django Reinhardt background to Jimmy's interpretation of Stephane Grappelli.

We also invited clarinet and sax man Ivan Tooes on a couple of occasions and we once had Peter Oxborough who also played clarinet and alto sax.

My daughter Elisabeth, who had studied drama under Ann Edwards, was able to come along to several concerts and provide some amusing readings which audiences seemed to enjoy, especially those of Joyce Grenfell. The school mistress one – "George, don't do that" – went down very well.

Elisabeth's long time friend Corena Lord joined us at one old folks' home to play her classical guitar with pieces by Rodriguez and other Spanish composers. She came along to Salhouse when we entertained at the harvest supper in the village hall, delighting all with her beautiful playing. Interestingly enough, Elisabeth was on the same bill that evening, as was Stan Ferrari.

On a number of occasions we invited David Perkins to sing, choosing his own songs such as 'September Song', 'The Twelfth of Never' and 'Speak Softly Love' with the odd dip into Gilbert and Sullivan such as 'Tit Willow'.

David was part of the company which entertained at Downham Market Town Hall during their festival week, where I also included Norma Wick and Gerry Morter ('Geraldini' the magician).

We played to a full house that night, Gerry rounding off both the first and second half with his quick-fire tricks and the irrepressible Norma leaving the audience in stitches with her own particular brand of humour.

Both Norma and David took part in a concert we did for St Barnabas's church centre when Reg Piesse asked us to organize the programme which was to be held on a Saturday evening in Princes Street church in Norwich. We also had Chris Speake along with Peter Winter agreeing to compere.

With a reasonable sized audience sitting waiting, Royle suddenly realised he hadn't collected Jimmy Skene and rushed off in his car to Eaton.

Clearly we had to make a start, which was when Peter Winter was supposed to announce an overture, a selection from a show by Tony and Jimmy (not music written by Tony and Jimmy but performed by them from a well-known one).

No Jimmy, so I went through the selection which he and I had so carefully practised, my filling in the violin bits on 'Roland'.

Shortly after, came something of a commotion when Norma walked on to the stage holding Jimmy's hand and saying to Peter and the audience:

"I found this little man in the alley looking for the place he was supposed to play his violin."

Laughter all round, of course, with Jimmy forgetting his dismay at Royle's amnesia and entering into the spirit of the whole evening. We had the services of Edward Murray-Harvey during the interval to play his barrel organ, delighting everyone; Peter Winter provided a comic song and a charming finale of operetta favourites rounded off a successful evening which raised money for such a good cause.

Jenny Hall asked me to bring a musical group for a 'special' supper at Blickling Hall where invited guests would be dining on gastronomic delights (but invited to pay for them).

I remember that on a very wet night, Royle, Miriam, Jimmy and I went along and set up in an oak-panelled room set out with dining tables. During dinner, Jimmy and I played show selections, after which the four of us entertained the 'guests' who had clearly dined (and wined) well.

We must have done well since we were asked back to a number of 'theme' nights when only our personnel changed. Chris Speake came as our guest for one night when I do remember his and Miriam's fine duet 'You Are Love' from Kern's *Showboat*.

Jimmy Skene invariably caused mildly amusing looks from audiences who saw before them a little, almost bald man, bespectacled and joined to his violin in deep reverie.

Apart from when he had to read some music, Jimmy's eyes were tightly shut as he apparently played in trance-like fashion.

As to his own appearance, by his own admission he likened himself to the funny little bald sidekick in the Benny Hill show, openly laughing about it and finding the whole thing utterly hilarious.

He had never appeared on television but he had appeared on stage in a series with organist Robin Richmond, entitled 'The organ, the monkey and me', when Jimmy, sitting on the organ, fiddled away dressed in a monkey costume!

When we did a big concert at Drayton Methodist Church as a fund raiser, we had Myra Bowles who sang 'Something Wonderful' from *The King and I*, Phil Penn who played some classic trumpet tunes and David Boast delighting everyone with some Rachmaninov at the piano. David also accompanied Miriam sing Dvorak's 'Song to the Moon' – music that I found had too many notes in it for me to handle.

We had a lively finale with an odd instrumental assortment – piano, violin and trumpet, beating out Strauss's 'Radetsky March' with the audience inevitably clapping their way through in the way of tradition.

Don Hoffmann joined us for a few afternoon shows, singing in his inimitable and powerful style. He would often meet up with someone in the audience he knew, such as at Long Stratton Day Centre where a great brick pillar made it difficult to see all your audience at the same time.

It must have been late in 1997, or possibly early 1998, when I began to notice faults in Jimmy's pitching, particularly in the high register which sometimes went wildly astray. You could see one or two raised eyebrows in the audience with the occasional wince and just a chance remark now and then.

Actually, Jimmy was aware of his loss of correct pitch which was certainly not helped by his hearing aid that did not pick up the harmonics. Defiantly he took himself off to the ear doctor who told him he had his hearing aid on backwards, something which couldn't have helped matters.

With the contraption on frontwards, things improved marginally, although I knew he wasn't hearing well, having to say "Pardon" with increasing regularity, sometimes before anyone had spoken.

I suppose it was amusing at lunch table at the Essex Rooms when Jimmy was asked a question such as:

"How long have you played the violin?"

He would answer: ''Yes, I love fish and chips.''

The pitching grew worse as Jimmy's hearing deteriorated, with my wondering what I could do for the best without hurting such a wonderful musician and friend. The solution to the problem came not from me but from Jimmy himself who one day said to me: "Tony, I'm afraid I shall have to hang up my violin. I'm not pitching correctly, I can't hear the middle and upper register notes properly and I don't want to be a liability to the group."

So there it was: he had made that decision which for Jimmy was final, although he did continue to play in the quiet of his own bedroom, possibly in the hope that the ear would improve.

Sad though it was, he knew be was right, as did I, for there is nothing worse than someone in the music world or entertainment business going on beyond their peak, creating embarrassment all round.

Dear Jimmy gave me one of his violin bows to hang in my study as a reminder of him and the happy times we had shared. The bow hangs there still.

Although he would come each week with me to the Essex Rooms for lunch and to listen to me with the various guest singers there, Jimmy never played again, although I know he must have yearned to do so.

"I've had a wonderful life," he would say, "doing what I loved best and getting paid for it. Who could want better than that?"

Who indeed?

Clearly I had to find a replacement, although Jimmy was certainly a hard act to follow from many points of view but a violinist seemed just right for our type of entertainment. When I asked John Winsworth to join us, he insisted that he was no solo violin player.

"Neither was Jimmy to start with," I said, "but look how he turned out."

Thankfully, John agreed to become one of Tony and Friends, joining me in the opening selection and playing a solo mid-way through the programme, which was sometimes in 'Karaoke' style with John leading a 'hidden' orchestra.

Two favourites here were Mozart's 'Eine Kleine Nachtmusik' (not all of it !) and Boccerini's 'Minuet' which I would tell the audience was featured in the Alec Guinness film *The Lady Killers*.

In between the violin pieces John would take up his bass guitar to accompany me, as I played medleys, taxing the memories of the senior citizens, some of who stayed awake.

Miriam took retirement from work in December 2000, leaving her able to sing with the daytime shift. We had discussed the 'when' of her retirement many times but our final resolve had been determined by the untimely death of our friend Don Hoffmann, who had collapsed at a party. He and Janet, his wife, had planned a quiet retirement together that never came and I was adamant that Miriam should take an early exit from work so that we might have some time together.

In addition, I could benefit from having her singing and cease being the 'bigamous' husband with an afternoon wife.

'Tony and Friends' mainly turned out as four on the bill with Miriam, John and Royle accompanying me or, I suppose, me accompanying them.

We had some very pleasant afternoons or evenings with scores of friends made along the way. The venues are too many to mention all, but we particularly continued to enjoy going to Jessopp Road, Poringland, Thorpe Vintage Club, Thorpe Evergreens, The Gothic Club, Doughty's Hospital, Foulger's House and Brundall.

Royle was always a great favourite with his 'Nobody Loves a Fairy When She's Forty' routine, more so when he grew a beard. He achieved the ultimate acclaim when he gave a complete solo act to the members of the Gothic Club when I was taken ill and could not appear. Being the great trouper we was, he even produced 'The Fairy' with her full costume over his other clothes which must have been quite bizarre.

There were places we went to that bear interesting comment such as

Albany House, Fakenham, where Miriam had to sing to two rooms and yes, Royle had to be the fairy in two places at once. Still, I suppose that is the 'magic' of show business. The Ogden Court lounge at Wymondham was huge and it would have been better for us had the audience assembled at one end, but many folk had their seats booked in a particular spot for the duration, some at the far end and that was where they intended to sit. Fine – except that during our performance we would here very audibly:

"What did he say?"

"I don't know – I can't hear what they're saying."

"I can't hear what she's singing."

And so on. You can't win.

At Gorleston we came upon a little lady pacing up and down in the foyer of the home.

"I'm waiting for my husband," she said. "He loves music and would so much enjoy your concert."

As the time for us to go on grew nearer, she seemed to grow more and more anxious, wringing her hands, saying: "Where can he be? Where has he got to?"

We performed our show in a lovely big lounge to a most receptive set of people but it was noticeable that the little lady did not appear, a point we mentioned to a nurse.

"It happens all the time," she said, "Her husband died eleven years ago."

As I have mentioned elsewhere in this book our group often had guest artistes and husband and wife Colin and Colleen Harris came along several times.

At Herondale at Acle, a lady staying there for a week or so threw a tantrum, coming from behind us to shower us with water from a large water jar. When her apparent rage reached its peak, she hurled the glass jar which flew over my left shoulder, dropping water as it went to crash to the floor on Colleen's left, in the middle of her song.

In that split second I fancied that the wet on my arm was blood, while Colleen, not surprisingly was momentarily stopped in her cadenza. Two carers rushed to the scene, the first to conduct the irate lady to the quiet room, the second to collect the water jar.

Incidentally, they have a caged budgerigar at Herondale which trills away from the moment the music starts which is like having Percy Edwards on the bill.

Colin and Colleen were with us at a Norwich rest home where a few surprises came our way. John Winsworth and I had only just commenced our show selection to open when a member of staff came between us with a vacuum cleaner – shades of Gerard Hoffnung. As Miriam sang her first solo

94

another member of staff decided to go round with a small basket selling raffle tickets, not the sort of thing you generally encounter at most opera houses.

The final insult was, when in Colleen's offering, yet another employee was openly demonstrating dresses and skirts to sell to the ladies in the audience, though mercifully not executing a cat-walk.

John, our violinist, ordinarily a most calm and placid musician (there are some) said, "When you realise you've given up a third of a day to come out for this, it makes you say I won't bother."

I knew what he meant, it was from that incident I decided to give the various venues marks out of ten, just as I had done with pianos in the days of yore, and I will leave the reader to guess what score I gave to the last mentioned home.

At another place, halfway through Royle's monologue, the wet fish man arrived outside, a signal for several of the audience to get up and buy their supper. John was again with us and seeing his facial expression I did wonder if we should be losing him.

"You win some, you lose some," was Royle's philosophy, and of course he's right. For every bad show you'll have ten good ones.

You got used to all the places we performed: ancient village halls with dusty corners, fading royal portraits and a sepia 'Stag at Bay' and black and white or sepia photographs of the village as it was in far off times, something that Miriam loved to see.

Some places still owned an ancient piano, occasionally bearing original candle-sticks, others with them removed, and invariably most of them showing years of wear and tear.

There were the many nursing homes, retirement places and sheltered houses, some luxurious, some like the curate's egg and others where you wouldn't put your worst enemy.

One of the worst aspects out in the country was actually finding the place, for there were rarely any signs, very few signs of human life to ask, and in the dark you could spend ages going round in circles before locating the home.

Many of the homes were very modern, light and airy, with a pleasant outlook, spacious communal lounge, beautifully decorated and furnished and having the best of carers and helpers. Others were so awful either because of the dreary premises or the lax personnel.

I remember one January, arriving in snowdrop time at a home in North Norfolk where, after penetrating the security system, I asked for Janet.

"She left last November – who are you, and what do you want?"

''We're the three entertainers booked by Janet for today."

Clearly, they knew nothing about it, since Janet had not 'passed on' any such thing, which meant that the residents' lounge was empty, no lunchtime concert being expected. One of the nurses said she would round up a few residents to get them down to the lounge while we set up, which sounded like a press-gang mission.

Miriam, Royle and I gave a one-hour show to these elderly people, one lady doing a bit of light capering about, touching Royle and me, but had to be restrained by a nurse when she began investigating the electrics for the keyboard.

Afterwards, as was usual, I was led to an office to collect expenses from a secretary who asked:

"Do you have an invoice?"

"I'm sorry, I haven't."

"I can't pay you without an invoice, you will have to send it."

We had come over forty miles with the prospect of another forty to return, had not been expected or prepared for, a half asleep audience had been hurriedly put into place and to cap it all we were offered no refreshment, not as much as a cup of tea.

I said: "Pay me and I'll send you a receipt."

The secretary replied: "Who shall I make the cheque to?"

A cheque!

As she wrote it, she turned to the nurse who had been in attendance at our concert and asked: "Were they any good?"

I nearly bit through my tongue, but said nothing, observed that she not wearing a charm-school medal and vowed to myself that we would not be back.

At Martham, the lady who ran the old folks' club had been their secretary for fifty years which I thought must be something of a record and suggested to her husband that he put his wife's name forward for Palace recognition. After all, they do seem to dish out gongs for far less.

Anne Hawkes joined us on a few occasions at Northfields, a home quite near Eaton Park in Norwich. She would read poems or prose, while Miriam provided the songs. One dear lady there would insist on using extremely colourful language to both Anne and Miriam, clearly venting her venom on womankind, for it was never cast in my direction. Once or twice she had to be taken to her room, since the expletives were coming thick and fast, which was not felt to be conducive to the proceedings in the lounge.

For a time, I went 'solo' to entertain and give my talk *Norfolk as She is Spoke* and another *The Music in My Life*, being an account of my musical career from a small boy to my retirement in 1989.

The very first of these was at Wensum Probus Men's Club which seemed to go down well enough for me to elaborate upon it by illustrating the presentation with my keyboard.

I was, by this time, using the more portable Technics which I could manage easily on my own.

It was at one such talk that a member of the audience suggested I should put all my musical experiences into writing which is how my first book *S'Wonderful* was born. I devised a third musical solo spot entitled *You Must Remember This* which was a programme of audience participation recalling signature tunes of radio programmes or personalities of a bygone age, another show that seemed to touch the imagination of audiences.

I brought Miriam into it to sing some of the music, such as 'With a Song in My Heart' from *Two Way Forces Favourites* (later *Two Way Family Favourites*) and following her retirement she was able to come with me during the afternoons.

With a programme like that I received a tremendous amount of feed-back, with so many snippets given to me by members of the audience, adding so much credence to the whole thing.

One lady told me that she had nursed Chesney Allen in a Norfolk nursing-home in his last days, while another told me she had encountered George Formby on her Broads holiday when she moored opposite *The Lady Beryl*.

A gentleman informed me that Eric Coates had been inspired to write 'By a Sleepy Lagoon' in 1930 with the view he had from Selsey across to Bognor Regis, the melody being used for Roy Plomley's *Desert Island Discs*.

Another pensioner told me that RAF Swanton Morley was the station upon which *Much Binding in the Marsh* was founded and that Richard Murdoch had been the entertainments' officer there at one time.

Into the list of early radio programmes I brought 'Devil's Galop', Charles Williams' tune for *Dick Barton – Special Agent*, remembered and loved by so many as is obvious from the faces of my audiences.

I would tell them how I would eagerly await the adventures of Dick, Jock and Snowy every evening, then castigating the BBC for taking it off and 'dumping it in the countryside', which was my signal to play 'Barwick Green', the tune of *The Archers*.

This always went down well, except on one very embarrassing occasion, when after my clear expression of disgust about *The Archers*, a lady stood up in the audience and said coldly:

''Do you mind! My father – Godfrey Baisley produced *The Archers*.''

It is that kind of moment when you wish the earth would open up and swallow you.

Of course there were many in my audiences who had seen some of the artists I recalled, either on stage or actually alongside them, such as the lady who worked for Jessie Matthews through to when she became Doctor Dale's wife in *Mrs Dale's Diary*, or the man who had met Max Miller on his last tour.

I played the signature tunes of many old programmes such as *Music While You Work*, *ITMA* (It's That Man Again), *Much Binding in the Marsh* and *In Town Tonight*, as well as those of individual artists such as Arthur Askey, Max Miller, Issy Bonn, Donald Peers, Arthur Tracy and Cavan O'Connor.

I did this performance at nursing-homes where the nurse or sister would remark that some residents who rarely opened their mouths were answering my musical questions and it was clear that music awakened memories for them. Many of the staff declared it was very therapeutic for the old people: such is the power of music.

The radio and stage programmes led to my compiling a second one, this time recalling the early days of television with musical snippets from black and white viewing. I led off with the theme from *Z Cars*, asking the name of the inspector and the actor who played him. Many members of the audience chorused: "Charlie Barlow – Stratford Johns."

I followed this with the tune to *Dixon of Dock Green* with questions about Jack Warner and his sisters, Elsie and Doris Waters.

After a great deal of research I compiled a long catalogue of TV programmes from the past that had an easily-recognizable signature tune or theme, all of which got the audience thinking and remembering.

To bring Miriam into the presentation, I brought her on to be a 'video', something most people put on when the 'live' television offers nothing worth watching.

Such videos were *Showboat*, *Oklahoma*, *Carousel* and *My Fair Lady*, not that she sang every song from each but chose 'Can't Help Lovin' That Man', 'People Will Say We're in Love', 'If I Loved You' and 'I Could Have Danced All Night'.

Audiences were very quick to remember names and programmes such as *The Onedin Line* with people telling me that the music was 'Sparticus' by Khachaturian; or *Alfred Hitchcock's Hour*, although rarely did anyone identify the music: 'Funeral March of a Marionette' by Gounoud.

Again, the popularity of the programme led me to devise another based upon music from the cinema with themes from all types of films – comedy, epics, drama, westerns, wartime and even children's.

I played themes from such films as *Born Free* closely followed by *Lawrence of Arabia*, this to show the similarity of the opening bars of John Barry's music and that of Maurice Jarre. There were the war films such as *The Great Escape* with its stirring march, with the ever-present side-drum beat, rather like *The Longest Day* that had a very similar idea, with even the identical opening notes.

Sir Malcolm Arnold's *Bridge on the River Kwai* being the counter melody of 'Colonel Bogey' was clever, while Eric Coates' fine music for *The Dam Busters* was stirring stuff, even though the Trio closely resembled a popular song of the time 'I'll Never Stop Loving You'.

In the Westerns there was a bit of fun in playing *The Magnificent Seven* quickly followed by *The Big Country* just to see how many of the audience named each correctly, since once again they do have similarities.

With the children's films everyone knew *Snow White* when I played 'Some Day My Prince Will Come', but only an occasional member would recognize 'When You Wish Upon a Star' as being featured in *Pinocchio*.

Some classic film dramas had music that was so closely associated with the story that when I played it, a smile of recognition would come on everyone's face.

The 'Harry Lime' theme was a good example where people would chorus: "*The Third Man*" and others like 'Moon River' from *Breakfast at Tiffany's* and 'The Entertainer' from *The Sting* were likewise acknowledged.

Audiences were quite surprised to learn that Lionel Bart wrote 'From Russia With Love' and that the script for *Brief Encounter* was the work of Noel Coward.

There was always plenty of feedback, things I learned in all my programmes, such as from the lady who told me that when *Lawrence of Arabia* was shown at her local cinema just before the interval (it was a very long film) where Peter O'Toole and Omar Sharif are crossing the burning desert with the sun blazing down, the management turned the heat up so that the audience demand for ice cream and drinks exceeded normal by far.

It was all great fun with so much to be gained from audience participation but, of course, where I gave regular presentations such as at my Wymondham Probus Club I had to devise something else. After all, there were only so many radio programmes, so many TV shows and so many films!

I hit on the idea of *The A to Z of Music*, making a comprehensive coverage of anything and everything associated with popular music in alphabetical form under the headings of people (artists, composers, lyricists), shows and songs. It was such a full list that I hardly made much progress from the letter A in the first talk, with names such as Fred Astaire, Julie Andrews and Louis Armstrong together with shows like *Annie Get Your Gun* and *Anything Goes* taking up a great deal of the allotted time, although this didn't seem to worry the Probus members at all.

One other talk I gave, with my keyboard to help, was about the dance bands and their leaders with each of the signature tunes, again as an opportunity for the audience to identify the tunes as well as the men. Some were quite easy such as Billy Cotton with 'Somebody Stole My Gal' and

Henry Hall's 'Here's to the Next Time' while others were less well known such as 'Say it With Music', Irving Berlin's song used by Jack Payne and his orchestra.

I shared with the audience my memories of dancing lessons to Victor Silvester (I do mean his records of course) like so many others of my generation, his tempo being perfect as his orchestra led us into the first quick-step 'Slow, slow – quick, quick, slow' with the tune 'You're Dancing on My Heart'. I remembered as a young man Victor's World Requests programmes when he would announce: "for Akimo Obanji of Dar-es-Salaam, the waltz 'I'm Dancing with Tears in My Eyes'," or; ''for Shenshi Hakanawa from Honshu the fox-trot 'Rip Tide'." I recall that weekly programme giving me some amusement as well as a feeling of incredulity that people from the four corners of the globe should be tuned in to Victor Silvester's western music, and also to request it.

In hindsight, I suppose I ought to have gone in for my 'one man shows' long ago which, had I done so, would have left me well-placed to obtain an Equity card, entitling me to small parts for various television series or even for my 'musical fingers' used in closeups! To be a mere musician alone did not give that entitlement which required you to be a performer, a fine distinction as the reader will discern and my efforts over the years to own the magic card had come to nothing.

The best of the concerts we gave under the heading of Tony and Friends were those at St Margaret's church, Drayton, in aid of church funds. In 1999 we decided to commemorate the centenary of the birth of George Gershwin, presenting a concert of his music and the lyrics of his brother Ira. The company included singers David Perkins and Miriam, with Matt Clark playing snatches of Gershwin compositions such as the theme from *Rhapsody in Blue*. I wrote and read the narrative, accompanied the songs backed by John Winsworth (double bass) and Joe Jenkins (drums) and devised the programme. The evening raised £300 for the church and was pronounced a great success.

The church committee asked us to come up with another concert the following year and in similar vein we did a tribute to Noel Coward, this time including Norma Wick, Colin Thackery and Ian ('Oz') Topliff in our company. My daughter Elisabeth danced in to 'Dance Little Lady' sung by Colin, while Norma and Ian provided such amusing numbers as 'I Went to Marvellous Party' and 'Don't Put Your Daughter on the Stage, Mrs Worthington', all of which delighted the large audience. After Colin's rendition of 'Sail Away', came the finale of 'I'll See You Again' with the audience joining in to round off another memorable evening.

That evening the narration of Coward's life was read by David Perkins who was recovering from a major operation and was not fit enough to be able to sing.

The folk at Drayton, delighted at the success of another venture, asked us to return in 2001. We duly obliged, opting for yet another composer – Cole Porter. I researched his life, slotting in the songs he had composed without help, for Porter, like Irving Berlin, Frank Loesser (*Guys and Dolls*) and Jerry Herman (*Hello Dolly*), did it all by himself, words and music, declaring: "Why use two or three others to write the lyrics when I can do it myself."

Again we had a hugely successful and satisfying evening with the church profiting by £500.

The centenary of the birth of Richard Rodgers in 2002 was a ready-made programme for the fourth Drayton concert in October. Colin Thackery researched the lives of Richard Rodgers, Lorenz Hart and Oscar Hammerstein, putting together a well-informed narrative which he delivered to a large audience. Our cast included Oz, David and Miriam, with Colin slipping in his contributions plus the duet with Miriam 'When the Children are Asleep' from *Carousel*.

Elisabeth, together with Jennie Bugg, danced 'Ten Cents a Dance' in the first half, while in the second they danced and sang 'I Cairn't Say No' from *Oklahoma*. I had Joe Jenkins on percussion again, and on double-bass was Richard LeGrice who gallantly stepped in at the last moment, literally, to deputise for John Winsworth, and well he accomplished the task (as I knew of course he would).

The finale was the audience joining the company in four songs from *The Sound of Music* which I felt was a fitting end to a good evening all round, saluting the life of man who ranks among the top musical writers of the twentieth century.

The 'Tony and Friends" group has lasted the course well with some excellent guest artistes joining us over the years, more recently to include Colin and Colleen Harris, Colin Thackery and Norma Wick, the last-named giving me plenty of 'stick' at the piano, though I hasten to add all in good jest, something she would deny vehemently.

I look back to those early days of the original Tony and Friends with the fondest affection, remembering the remarkable Jimmy Skene, eyes shut tight as his violin bow danced its way through Kreisler's 'Schoen Rosmarin'. I can hear Vi and Ernie Shaves in duet, and see Ernie's odd little capers as a song finished, while the incredible exploits of Albert, Sam and the others in monologues echo through the north country tones of Royle Drew.

Added to those things were the delightful and romantic songs as put over by Miriam, now my wife, and you have a sextet of quality, enjoyed by so many audiences that asked us to return time and again.

I remember the good places and the bad, the big halls and the small dimly-lit ones, such as the tiny theatre at the top of the Bystanders' Club off Thorpe Road. You had to reach it by some break-neck stairs which led to a miniscule stage and tiered seats for, I suppose, about 60 people. At the back of these seats was a door which I remember opening to reveal a sheer drop to the concrete below, a feature which caused Miriam some consternation. There was a piano – about 6 out of 10 – though how it was ever brought up there gave me cause to wonder.

There is so much to remember of those days that bring a wistful smile to the members of the group that are left, when 'Tony and Friends' billed as *Music, Laughter and Song* set out to make people 'forget their troubles and wear a smile'.

I wouldn't have missed it for worlds.

CHAPTER TEN

Will Ye No Come Back Again?

WHEN I ran the renowned Rémon Quartet in the 'Fifties and 'Sixties and we played in what was then termed High Society, we invariably had to play Scottish dances such as 'The Dashing White Sergeant' and 'Strip the Willow', not easy with our line-up of piano, drums, sax and bass.

From a secondhand shop in Charing Cross (the Norwich one, not the London borough) I purchased a small accordion which I duly handed to Dennis Payne, my bass player, asking him to practise it until he became our Jimmy Shand.

Very soon he became proficient, not quite Jimmy Shand but close, and we began to sound like a Scottish Country dance band which delighted the dancers.

The dreaded cry was: "More" or "Encore" when Dennis's fingers and mine had to perform further gymnastics through endless rounds of reels – making us reel (ghastly pun).

'Strip the Willow' would go on interminably until you had older folk appealing to you to stop, clearly suffering exhaustion.

In the Eightsome Reel the biggest problem we had was knowing when to finish, since there was rarely an MC to let you know. With Dennis on his accordion we ploughed our way through dozens of dances until close to the end of the days of the Rémon Quartet, the accordion's bellows suffered a 'cock-a-leaky' and it breathed its last. Maybe it was the very harbinger of the band's demise.

No more would I play those finger-scorching reels and jigs, as dancers swirled around the ballroom to near collapse – or would I ?

Some thirty years later I received a telephone call from a lovely lady called Ellen Clark who told me she was in office as the new president of the Norfolk and Norwich Caledonian Society and needed – yes, a Scottish Country Dance band to play at the St Andrew's Night Dinner Dance.

Now Ellen couldn't have known of the Rémon Quartet, long since gone, nor could she have known of my Scottish origins, since I didn't learn of those myself until some nine years later.

So why the call, and why me ? I shall never know but doubtless somebody had given her my name as being just the chap to conjure up a Scottish sounding outfit.

Luckily for me the redoubtable James Skene, Esquire, was extremely versatile and thoroughly versed in anything north of the border, musically speaking that is, being able to busk 'The Flowers of Edinburgh', 'The Devil Among the Tailors' and dozens more.

It was also useful that he could speak the language fluently and able to give me any quick translations I might need.

Next I needed a Jimmy Shand, a squeezebox man to add authenticity to the Scottish sound. Did I know such a man ? Well, of course I did: my longtime friend Joe Dade, at that time appearing daily in the St Stephen's underpass in Norwich, in French attire, busking his way through a thousand tunes to delight the passing shoppers. Joe didn't read music but then neither did the great Jimmy Shand, both men busking their way through life with apparent ease and in complete control of their instruments.

The quartet would be completed by percussion giant, big Don Brewer, a highly experienced drummer who could manage a song or two in the 'English' dances.

Ellen Clark was on tenterhooks about that first night of her presidency with maybe a degree or so of unease about the band – my band. Was it to be Tony MacIreland and His Scottish Country Dance Band or perhaps Hamish and the Cockaleekies?

The changes in band and orchestra names over the years have been remarkable.

In the 'Thirties we had Jack Hylton and His Orchestra, Carroll Gibbons and the Savoy Orpheans and even Carroll Gibbons and His Boy Friends – can you imagine that one today? And there was the Billy Cotton Band Show.

Collective nouns abounded and then the more recent things developed like Ricky Moron and the Layabouts, which soon dropped the Ricky Moron bit to become The Layabouts. Very soon the plural became singular and we have Layabout; I think it's called progress. In the published pop charts I can never be sure whether I'm reading the name of the number or the name of the group or vice versa and please – let's not call them bands, particularly when they don't or can't actually play anything.

Anyway, I was not listed in the smart programme as anything more fancy or fanciful than 'The Tony Ireland Band'.

The supper dance was held in the hall of Trinity United Reform Church, Unthank Road, and I took along my Casio keyboard, I remember, on which I played through the meal.

Afterwards, we four ploughed our way through the reels, 'Dashing White Sergeant' and 'Gay Gordons', as well as the 'English' dances – quickstep, waltz and what used to be called the slow fox-trot.

Ellen Clark need never have worried, since the whole thing was an unqualified success with praises lavished all round. As for the band: will you play for us again ?

Hence the title of this very chapter.

Each year brought a new president of the Caledonian Society and following on in 1993 it was the turn of Edward ('Ted') Purser, who like most of his successors appeared to go around like a cat on hot bricks and carrying the troubles of the world on his shoulders.

Our venue changed to the Hotel Norwich, starting with the St Andrew's Night in November, followed by Burns' Night in January when we were still billed as The Tony Ireland Band. By now I had bought 'Roland', a super electric piano having a full grand piano sound and length of keyboard. It weighed a ton, needing my sack barrow to transport it and Roland became a part of the outfit, even the dancers addressing him affectionately as 'Roland'.

Getting to the City Suite at the hotel meant going round to the tradesmen's entrance where you had to identify yourself before unloading all the band gear, Roland included of course, into a lift which was often piled with food trays and a trolley or two.

Like many other lifts I have encountered it was temperamental, having an annoying habit of closing at the most inconsiderate moments or refusing to ascend when asked.

Of course at the Burns' Night, we had a piper to pipe in the haggis and we would be aware of his imminent entry as we listened to him gathering the air into his bag (or should it be bellows?) from behind us.

My violinist, Jimmy, was a most unorthodox and somewhat irreverent Scot, detesting the 'skirl' of the pipes, which he considered best heard on a hilltop several miles away, preferably out of ear-shot.

The piper would parade to top table, closely followed by the head chef bearing the haggis which was set before the president.

There would follow the ceremony known as 'addressing the haggis' involving someone as orator delivering Burns' ode to the same with a dirk plunged into it at some point. At the conclusion of the ode, the chef and the piper would be presented with a glass of whisky, the Scottish national beverage, yet another of Jimmy's dislikes.

The ode itself was in Burns' own Gallic style which we English musicians found mainly unintelligible, though I suspect that a fair number of the invited audience were not well-versed in the tongue either. Certainly it was of no use asking Jimmy to translate the words, since his description of the bard's words do not bear repeating and you will recall I did say Jimmy was a very unorthodox Scot.

While I played background dinner music, the guests tucked into mounds of steaming haggis with 'neeps' and 'tatties', which to the uninitiated means turnips and potatoes. Clearly some of the diners did not find haggis to be counted among their gastronomic delights, judging by the returned plates to the kitchens, and neeps and tatties were not the ambrosia of the gods either.

After supper there followed speeches, some of which went on considerably with some guests visibly nodding off, wakened only by sporadic applause or by laughter from others who had remained awake to catch a funny line.

More often than not, the function was attended by the Lord Mayor or the Sheriff who would add to the list of speeches, all time-consuming which tended to curtail the amount of dancing the guests would have.

We'd sit in the adjoining lounge, passing the time in idle musicians' chat until we were told that speeches were over and dancing could begin.

Among the dancers there were some who were highly au fait with the Scottish steps and routines, such as Doug and Nancy Stewart, who I remember put everyone through their paces in the 'Cumberland Reel'. It was most useful having them in a set near us to start with, so as to begin correctly, but even more useful to have them nearby in such as the Eightsome Reel, so as to know when to finish!

Highly knowledgeable of Scottish dance etiquette was Alec Walker, who would complain bitterly about step faults and also bars missed out in the Scottish Country Dance (a waltz sequence). He would "tut tut" regularly, shaking his head in disapproval.

The dance couple who caught the eye were Ian and Marcia Fraser, a husband and wife partnership with superb footwork, which they showed best in things like the quickstep or fox-trot. They were the musicians' dream, first on the floor, smiling at the band as if showing their pleasure at the music and primarily encouraging everyone else to get up and dance.

My wayward Scot, Jimmy, was ever desirous to learn to 'speak properly' with the hope that local folk would understand him, rather than class him as an unintelligible 'foreigner' from somewhere up north.

At his request I became his elocutionist, attempting to get him to enunciate clearly in a kind of BBC English (or what used to be such) and to speak slowly and deliberately.

I didn't actually use "How now, brown cow" or "The rain in Spain…" but I did try hard to improve his diction and lose some of his Scottish gabble.

However, as soon as we arrived at any Caledonian function, Jimmy was immediately surrounded by several Scottish clans, greeting him thus: "Hullo Jimmy, fie ye dein?"

This was the signal for Jimmy to lapse into the Gallic vernacular with the greatest enthusiasm and in a matter of minutes all my speech lessons went out of the window, while he and his fellow countrymen exchanged pleasantries in a language generally heard north of Berwick on Tweed.

In the Caledonian's Jubilee year of 1994 their president was renowned Norfolk farmer Gavin Patterson, a busy and efficient man who insisted on everything being just so – and quite right too.

To my great surprise he spoke in Norfolk dialect with no trace of Scottish, easily explained, since it was a previous generation of Pattersons that had moved from Scotland to Norfolk to farm cattle.

The Society decided to have a President's supper and dance in June at Worstead Village Hall – Worstead being the home of the Pattersons and their farms. I had the same line-up, plus Miriam as a guest singer.

It was a splendid evening with a barbecue supper, great dancing with, I recall, a highly vigorous 'Strip the Willow'.

I was surprised and delighted to see Stan Sinclair, my former headmaster at Thorpe Hamlet School, there with his wife Olga, who entered into the frenetic proceedings with customary gusto, even demanding an encore of 'The Dashing White Sergeant' when everyone else seemed to be dropping, including us.

It seemed as though we were now firmly established as the Caledonians' resident band, playing for St Andrew's nights, Burns' nights and the President's supper dance, though never for Hogmanay at St Andrew's Hall in Norwich where they always booked a London band.

The Caledonian programme never varied much, though we did have a change of venue on a couple of occasions when they booked the banqueting room at Norwich City Football Club, which was fine, apart from trying to communicate with the dancers round huge pillars.

On one of these gigs I had Tony Wilkins on drums, a most polished and professional musician as well as a most likeable man, whom I had first met playing for Paul Donley at The Oaksmere at Eye.

In 1995, the quiet and charming Matthew Mitchell was in the president's chair with Burns' Night at the Hotel Norwich and St Andrew's at Norwich City's Executive Suite. Matthew had taken a shine to Miriam, or her voice (or both), and asked her to sing some Scottish songs at the St Andrew's night.

I remember she included 'Aye Fond Kiss', 'The Eriskay Love Lilt' and 'Westering Home' which delighted everyone.

Sometimes in the business you come across a great master of ceremonies, a rare specimen these days, but such a man was Rob Stevens, Norfolk farmer and former international rugby player (Scotland of course).

At the Hotel Norwich his powerful voice probably reached the Grampians, or at least Mousehold Heath, which almost made dancing obligatory to all.

Moreover, Rob knew his Scottish dancing, directing sets to begin with, before launching himself into the fray, having made sure that everyone knew what they were supposed to be doing.

Sometimes the reels would bring forth a great deal of whooping, which I suppose must date back to ancient Gallic war cries when clan met clan or Scot met sassanach in combat.

Jane Cargill was the chosen president for 1996, again from the Norfolk farming fraternity, a lovely lady fully resolved to make a great success of her Burns' Night at Hotel Norwich.

However, she had not bargained for the ultra verbosity of the speech makers, with a Scottish historian giving a biopic of Burns which lasted an hour, only to be followed by a Norwich dignitary launching into a soap-box diatribe, taking the speechifying to eleven o'clock, a total of two hours.

This left time for three quarters of an hour for dancing, giving rise to considerable anger among the paying guests who had, they argued, come to a dinner dance. You will imagine that we had sat it out for two hours, bored out of our minds, waiting.

We felt sorry for everyone, most of all Jane, though clearly the fault was not of her making.

Officially, I retired from the Scottish scene that year but Elsa Heighton persuaded me to continue and since her husband David had been at Norwich School like me, I could hardly refuse.

Sadly, Jimmy Skene had hung up his fiddle so I knew things could never be quite the same but into the kilted arena stepped John Winsworth.

John, like Jimmy, amplified his violin to play the reels and so forth, reading them, since he was no busker.

For the 'English' dances John would revert to a double-bass, a tremendous boost to the group which consisted of me on my new Technics keyboard, Joe Dade as ever on accordion and Joe Jenkins on drums.

For Elsa it was a most successful year, she putting in a lot of hard work assisted by her friend Aileen Grant who would follow her in the chair.

Did I then retire? No, I did not because Aileen persuaded me otherwise, just as Alec Mason did again in 1999. I seem to go to say "No" but out comes "Yes" – something I'm told I do quite often.

Same band, same venue, same dances with no different name: still dancing to The Tony Ireland Band. All that changed was the president, who in 2000, was none other than David Heighton, Elsa's husband. Now could I refuse an Old Norvicensian? No, of course not.

But it was the last time the quartet gathered together for the Caledonians because the following year with Moira Dye as president, we cut to two – Joe Jenkins on drums and me on keyboard at Reepham Town Hall.

Admittedly, it was a night of torrential rain for the president's supper, but numbers had been falling for some while and, despite the brave faces of Moira and treasurer David Strachan, I could see a decline within the society.

We'd had some great nights over the years with some wonderful people who had kept alive Little Scotland in Norfolk with the Tony Ireland Band helping the traditional music along.

I felt that my mother, with her Scottish ancestral connections, would have been proud.

"Will ye no come back again?" I hear whispered from time to time and I remember the words of my dear friend Jimmy Skene.

"Never go back, Tony, never go back."

CHAPTER ELEVEN

The Old Folks At Home

S EVERAL people soon discovered that I had retired in 1989, something which seemed to spread like wildfire. It was reminiscent of the song: 'I heard it on the grapevine', that mysterious network to which so many people seem to tune in to.

One such former music colleague was David Blyth, alias David Valentine (or perhaps the other way round) who had been vocalist with the Rémon Quartet in the late 'Fifties.

David himself had retired from his council job to form *The Valentine Show*, an all-singing, all-dancing act, currently touring the geriatric circuit at venues around Norfolk.

If I remember correctly, I joined him in company with Jimmy Skene, with Miriam adding her ten penneth when she was not at work.

In those seemingly far off days of the Rémon Quartet, David had been a successful vocalist, winning the acclaim of many, especially the fair sex with his ballads in the style of many good singers of the day, above all that of Dickie Valentine, his 'hero'.

Although the timbre of David's singing voice, not surprisingly in thirty-plus years, had lost much of its former quality, he himself carried that same charisma that had charmed the young ladies who had flocked around him. You could see the old folk, hearts a flutter, gazing in adoration, wanting David to woo them personally with a love song, and note – I am referring to the ladies! Just as he had had the birds coming out of the trees in his youthful days, so he did that with so many elderly ladies, some in frames and others in wheelchairs, as he traversed the room with his mike.

They loved it, with so many having the urge to take his hands and dance, though some of them unable to do so, but only sit and let him move their hands up and down in time with the music.

Right round the county we went from nursing homes to sheltered housing, from hospitals to luncheon clubs, David fronting the show, leaving Jimmy and me to play the music.

Jimmy would find it hilarious that many of the residents were younger than he was although I know a huge number of them thought he was 'an incredible little man'. His levity grew with the gigs and he would ass around in Monti's 'Czardas', shouting "Oy!" as he leapt up, still playing at high speed in the vivace bits.

David encouraged him to sing, if that's what it actually was, and Jimmy practised for a long while to perfect his own version of 'You Made Me Love You' in Gallic. He would take his violin under his arm, make his way to a likely old lady, get down on one knee and serenade her with his song in the most corvine way with totally unintelligible words. It generally caused convulsive laughter all round, including the nursing staff.

Mention of the staff, reminds me that David would get them to judge the 'best smile' as he delivered his own version of 'A Certain Smile'. This caused great delight and became a feature of almost every programme. The 'best smiles' came from the lady residents, who would beam at everyone from ear to ear, perhaps expecting some reward or other, which might even be a quick peck from the 'master'.

David had one or two guests to come and swell the party such as Jimmy Beaumont who would not only play his guitar but contribute a song or two, perhaps the quaint ramblings of 'The Singing Postman' being ever popular.

Jimmy found a jazz friend in the other Jimmy, with the two of them playing the roles of Django Reinhardt and Stephane Grappelli ad lib while I followed them to the finish. Whether or not the octogenarian-plus audiences appreciated it I don't know, but they seemed to tap along with numbers like 'Sweet Georgia Brown' and 'Who's Sorry Now ?'

Another guest of David's was Stan Baines who would come in around half an hour after we'd started armed with a sheaf of music, launching in with about eight or nine songs which invariably began with 'Chattanooga Shoe Shine Boy' plus 'Chattanooga Choo Choo'. Following those came ballads sung at just about the slowest pace I have ever heard causing Jimmy Skene to ask me :

"Is this what they call rubato, Tony ?"

Actually Stan had a good voice for a man in his 'eighties, himself a veteran of Dunkirk and a member of that association.

Stan arranged for *The David Valentine Show* to appear at the Dunkirk Veterans' dinner at the Lansdowne Hotel in Norwich, which included Miriam to sing and me to accompany and also play through dinner, assisted of course by Jimmy Skene.

One of the songs that Miriam chose was 'Vienna, City of My Dreams', which was taken up by war veteran Arthur Brough, rendering it in German, making it an unusual duet to say the least.

It was a successful evening, apart from the complaints from the veterans about the hotel charges, particularly in the drinks department, which tended to take the shine off the proceedings.

The venue for the following year was changed to Dunston Hall, the function being spoiled by long speeches which left small time for dancing and entertainment on a miniscule floor area.

So what of the repertory tour of the country retirement homes? *The Valentine Show* went to all points of the compass, where the reception would range on a temperature gauge from pleasantly warm to decidedly cool, although using that allusion to temperature with regard to the rooms we worked in, most were definitely tropical.

At Burgh, near Aylsham we went to do a Christmas party, which I have to say began quite disastrously and ended in mayhem.

Jimmy and I opened the evening with our medley 'A tribute to Ivor Novello', but hardly were we into 'Shine through my dreams' than the somewhat officious chap in charge said to David: "This isn't what we want at all. We're not in our dotage you know."

I believe that David thought he was joking at first, but no, he wasn't, and I took exception to his remarks on three counts: we'd hardly started the concert, Ivor Novello was of their vintage and his comments were rude, offensive and I felt, very sad, since they intimated that Ivor Novello was passé.

Things got worse and poor Miriam, due to sing some light operatic and show songs, said: "I want to go home"

Alcoholic beverage abounded with the result that several of the ladies began to abuse that title, making more than cow eyes at David, more like making a complete exhibition of themselves.

The evening ended with the residents, mostly in their cups, doing rock and roll to Christmas carols, presumably their idea of Yuletide festivities. The amazing thing was that everyone seemed to have had an enjoyable evening (Miriam being the exception), thanking us profusely for the 'lovely music', though I suspect it was the drink talking.

At Badgers' Wood in Drayton, I remember the awkward-shaped room with the white-wood piano set against a wall near the door. I remember too the incessant 'bleep' from an alarm that punctuated every song, every number and I remember those residents who wailed or cried habitually to interrupt the entertainment – though I didn't think we were that bad.

One of the things I recall vividly about many of these places of which I

Above: *Ad Hoc's* Wizard of Oz.

Below: *The Ad Hoc's* Oliver.

Norma Wick in former days.

Above: *Drummer Joe Jenkins.*

Below: *'Girls' from the Essex Rooms.*

Above: *Vi and Ernie Shaves.*

Below: *Yare Valley Jazz – BBC Radio Norfolk, 1994.*

Above: *Jimmy Skene.* Below, left: *Frances Chaplin and Betty Phillp.*

Below, right: *Elisabeth Ireland.*

Colin Thackery, Maddermarket Theatre, 1988.

Nobody Loves a Fairy – Royle Drew.

Above: *The Singing Seniors – Somerfield Supermarket 1998.*

Below: *Vintage Club 2000.*

write, is that on our arrival we might find a member of cleaning staff with a vacuum cleaner working in the lounge; a few residents dotted around, who would look up and say:

"What have we got some entertainment today?"

or,

"What are we going to have a singalong?"

It would be patently obvious no one was prepared for any entertainment so that on many occasions there were hurried arrangements made to drag an audience in, willing or otherwise.

David seemed to laugh all this off with nonchalance, but I found it annoying that whoever was in charge, had neither remembered anyone was coming, nor made any preparation for the residents or us.

Very often David would bring a massive amount of electrical equipment, with enormous speakers plus great lengths of cable, and I recall a little old lady blundering over some of it at Brooke House one afternoon.

Antagonism and aggression was in evidence at Coltishall Hall, where in an enormous Victorian lounge, everyone's seat was earmarked, every resident having his or her place 'set in stone' and woe betide if anyone sat in another's chair.

However, there were some sweet ladies there who proffered their warm congratulations to Miriam and me when we told them of our impending wedding.

I had an amazing incident at East Harling where I was due to meet David and Jimmy Beaumont for a lunchtime entertainment for an old folks' club. I drove into the village where, just across the road from the lovely old church, I spied a hall with lots of parked cars. I parked the car, approached the large hall, peering in through the partially curtained windows where I saw a great many elderly people and tables laden with food.

What I couldn't see was how to get in and therefore made my way round to a small door which was open. Beyond was a lady clearly engaged in coping with a mountain of washing up.

"Excuse me," I said, "but is this where they are expecting some entertainment?"

"I shouldn't think so, my dear," she replied, "this here's a funeral."

It was clear I had the wrong hall.

The Hawthorns home for the elderly on Unthank Road in Norwich, saw a change of ownership and three changes of matrons during the time we went there, though I hasten to add not in one visit. It stands out for a number of reasons: a lady with a hoover, vacuuming the lounge when we arrived, who like so many others was not aware we were coming. A summer garden party that lasted well into the evening after a 2.30pm start with our entertainment resembling something of a marathon. And lastly, the occasion on which David, searching around for someone to pay him travelling expenses, was told that the person able to execute such a transaction was not available and could he (David) come back tomorrow?

Considering that David was separated from the Hawthorns by about six miles, he could be justified in complaining of such treatment, for a mere thirty pieces of silver (well, £30 to be exact), he was more annoyed to find that they would not pay him £10 extra for the additional hours we had done.

It was at Larchwood on Yarmouth Road, Thorpe, that we met Mr Holmes, David's uncle and a former master carpenter with Riley's, a renowned Norwich builder. Mr Holmes was now a widower, having lost his wife the previous year, and had decided to leave his Thorpe bungalow and move into Larchwood.

One of the staff nurses at Larchwood was the second wife of the late Brian Green, who had led the famous Dixielanders in the mid 'Fifties when I had been his pianist.

At Lakenfields, off City Road, we encountered a female barber shop group who asked David if they could 'do a number', a kind of practice run, as they had only just been together for a short while. David, kind hearted as ever, agreed, with the result that they took over the entertainment for the next forty minutes, with not one, but a dozen or so numbers, leaving us to finish the evening. I did recall my old and trusted maxim: "Don't accept amateurs at all costs, or even no cost."

We had the same thing happen at The Limes, just off the Drayton High Road.

I bashed out – yes, bashed out some tunes on a piano that was a disgrace to its maker, to a noisy crowd of residents and families, after which David began to croon a few songs. Very shortly he was joined by a young lady who launched into a medley of jazzy numbers that seemed to go on, and on. Added to this was her fairly blatant attempt to seduce David with suggestions about nipping off into Norwich to do 'a spot of clubbing'.

David, not taking her invitation terribly seriously, chuckled away at her every word and seemed to be more attracted to the table of food that had been laid out at the side of the room. I don't remember exactly what ensued but maybe she left to go clubbing on her own, leaving David (and us) to scoff sausage rolls and vol-au-vents.

Some nursing homes were formally country houses that had been adapted for the purpose, such as the Manor, just outside North Walsham. It was a beautiful place, surrounded by lawns and approached by woodland filled with rhododendrons.

There, the residents gathered in the dining room to be wooed by David, to listen to Jimmy Skene's magic violin and to me playing some selection or other, in the first instance on the tiny ship's piano but later on my Roland.

The ship's piano had been presented to the home by an ex-naval officer and I remember it opened by pulling the front lid and then lifting it to reveal no more than four octaves.

In our audience was a delightful lady who had been on the musical stage, having danced with C B Cochran as a professional. Her party piece was 'Tea for Two' which she would sing in most charming way, every time we were there. An old gentleman, dubbed 'The Colonel' used to come in for the first part of our concert but leave when he felt the moment was right. His was a fantasy world, for he believed he owned the Manor and that the nurses and helpers were his 'staff', something they willingly subscribed to in order to humour him.

There were two other country houses which had become homes just like the Manor. One was at Scole, where there was a beautiful Bechstein grand, the property of the owner and which stood proudly in the main stairwell where we performed. I do recall that Miriam, desirous of playing upon this mighty instrument, practised a piece of Chopin diligently until she felt she was ready for 'a public performance'. This she would have done had it not been for two extremely rude and inconsiderate women who decided to talk all through the opening of our concert, which made Miriam withdraw from her venture – a great pity!

The other great country house was Saxlingham Nethergate Hall, off the beaten track, set in lovely grounds with a superb view from all sides. A resident of the home was a lady who had been an opera singer and a chanteuse of German lieder who would offer to sing something from her repertoire during the afternoon. She was clearly a very professional lady and although now quite elderly, could deliver a song in a most accomplished way.

She struck an affinity with Miriam, giving praise to her singing and showed her the apartment she had in the beautiful Elizabethan manor. Whether or not her vocal contributions were always acceptable to the rest of the residents I'm not sure, since some of her songs were in German and may not have been fully understood, or appreciated, by those non-opera fans, or those not fluent in German.

Another resident there was Fred Barnard, former long-time friend of my father's and once headmaster of what was known as The Open Air School in Norwich, where delicate children went to be educated. I had met him many years before when he was officiating as a Red Cross leader at two charity balls, one at Heydon Hall and the other at Wolterton Hall where my quartet provided the dance music. Mr Barnard was charming, always smiling and enjoying the music and singing, even though in his mid 'nineties confined to a wheel chair. He showed us his room upstairs which had a fine view of meadows and trees with sheep and cattle grazing. He had a radio, a television and other creature comforts, all of which, together with his bed, food and nursing, cost him £700 per week. Mr Barnard died at 97, and somehow Saxlingham Nethergate home never seemed quite the same again.

On about our last visit there David brought Jimmy Skene from Eaton while I came from Kirstead to meet them and we three gave a concert, on this occasion Miriam being at work, unable to join us.

At the end of the afternoon, as soon as we had packed away our gear, David went to find someone in order to collect our expenses but the owner didn't seem to be about. Eventually I left, with Jimmy waiting in David's car while David made a tour of the house, hoping to find someone who could give him his expenses.

Apparently, according to Jimmy he was gone for almost an hour which caused Jimmy, a man in his 'eighties, great distress. David eventually found the boss, only to learn that he had no money on him and had run out of cheques. The delay was furthered by the man himself popping off to the nearest bank for a new cheque book to return and sign one for David, by which time it was late and poor Jimmy was in quite a state.

But what organization! David had wanted a mere thirty or so pounds for a pre-planned entertainment which the home must have been aware of, yet he had had to grub around for over an hour to get paid. And for this, Mr Barnard and others had been paying £700 a week !

Miriam joined us when we went to Roxley House on the Yarmouth Road at Thorpe where we straightaway encountered a familiar sound of radio 'monkey music' blaring out to extremely elderly residents which didn't seem at all appropriate and I wouldn't have thought much good for their ears or their souls, poor things.

During the entertainment one elderly gent decided he was going 'walk-about', heading off through the kitchen door straight for the traffic-laden Yarmouth road. Fortunately, Miriam, having seen him go, went after him and persuaded him that the entertainment wasn't that bad and that for his health's sake, should return to endure the remainder of the show.

At Yew Tree House at Swainsthorpe we found Ted Cutler's wife Doreen. Ted had been a well-known pianist on the concert party scene and although we rarely met (pianists don't meet much), I knew him as a quiet man and splendid piano man. Doreen was a resident at Yew Tree House, having been there some time after Ted's death. She was pleased to chat and even volunteered a song or two.

There were two Sunnycrofts at Taverham, though I'm not exactly sure why. It was probably split into two sites with residents in one differing from the other because of their degree of care requirement. Each home had an electronic keyboard, one first-rate and the other around fifth-rate, though why I don't know. David and I queried the fact but I don't remember any conclusive answer and the fifth-rate one remained, with its ineffectual sounds and a tendency to wheeze.

Just along the road from Sunnycroft was Two Acres, one and two for probably the same reason as Sunnycroft. It was there that, where we entertained lay right in the path of the route to the nurses' rest room, which meant that every so often a nurse or two would have to walk through the performers either to or from their quiet place which we did admit was slightly disconcerting.

There was a lovely grand piano at Brooklyn House at Attleborough, standing in the main foyer. I was delighted to be able to play it but unfortunately it was too wide to go into the residents' lounge which meant they had to strain their ears to listen. Other than that I used my Casio keyboard in the lounge itself but I must say it was great to play the beautiful grand, even though my audience couldn't see me and I couldn't see them. A bit like radio I suppose.

Woodlands Nursing Home at Hellesdon, where my mother-in-law had died, had the smallest of lounges into which they crowded as many people as possible to be entertained, using a shoe horn to squeeze three of us into one corner, namely Miriam , David and me. Of course, if a fourth came along in the person of Stan Baines, then it meant taking turns to breathe.

Into this tiny apartment dear David incorporated amplification which presumably benefitted anyone who had not been crammed in with us or even members of the public happening to pass the home.

The lounge at Tudor Grange, Wroxham, was larger and housed fewer people in our audience but did include a canary (in a cage I hasten to add) which added its own individual descants to our music, which either improved things or not, depending on your point of view.

One of the residents there, a Welshman called David (well – what else?) could wend his way through 'Sospan Fa' in Welsh of course, at break-neck speed to everyone's delight. His encore was to reel of the name of the longest railway station sign in Wales (or anywhere) – known to the English as Llanfair PG. All this effort would exhaust David, who would sit back beaming at everyone, aglow with the success of his contribution.

An interval came with a cup of tea and a rest for the Valentine show, plus the canary. After tea the canary began again with David (Valentine) serenading the old ladies and taking some of them by both hands in a sitting position (they, not him). Naturally enough, sleep would overcome some of the residents, lulled by the dulcet tones of the artistes, together with the often overpowering heat in the room, even in summer.

Paul Eden (alias Roger Blanchflower), a gentle giant of a man with a thunderous voice, joined David and me on a couple of occasions, although I had met him originally at the Pier Hotel, Gorleston when he had entertained at the Essex Rooms outing and I had been his ad hoc accompanist.

Paul sang with such power that you got the impression he had his own built-in amplification system, although he was able to use his control switch to produce pianissimo when necessary.

He was with us at Three Towers in Mile Cross, Norwich, where he delighted his audience with a variety of songs which included a dynamic 'La Reve Passe' (The Soldier's Dream) and ended with 'Goodbye' from *The White Horse Inn*.

Now at that time I was feeling desperately unhappy, having lost my lovely wife Jane and feeling utterly alone, miserable and not sure whether or not I wanted to go on.

In his programme Paul included a song called 'The Last Farewell' by Roger Whittaker and one that was generally sung by him. The words of the song ran :

"For you are beautiful
And I have loved you dearly
More dearly than the spoken word can tell."

Our interval followed this number and with those words filling my mind, I slipped into an adjoining empty room and wept bitter tears.

When I returned, I was offered a cup of tea and sat next to a dear little lady who said : "What's the matter, dear ? You've been crying."

Without inhibition I poured out my soul to her, a complete stranger, telling her all that had befallen me and how I still grieved.

"I know what you mean, dear," she said, "but life is for living – you cannot live with the dead."

Her words stayed with me, not only just then but remained in my heart for a long time, to come to give me comfort and a greater hope. The bitter sweet words of Paul's song had made me cry copiously but the old lady's words had helped to dry my tears to give me fresh hope.

The Valentine show went all over Norfolk, from village to small town, from a tiny hamlet to a seaside resort, with far too many places to name individually but all the time having the sole purpose of making elderly folks' lives happier.

Of course, occasionally you might sense that they were not happier with little clues like leaving the room not to return, sticking fingers in their ears or deciding to sing their own impromptu rendering which might have indicated some disapproval.

One jolly old fellow, known simply as 'Tan', resident at Brundall Nursing Home would suddenly break into song – a saucy sea shanty, which he might repeat several times during the afternoon. He would follow this by the loud declaration: "Soon my Heavenly Father is going to call me and I shall be with my beloved Margery."

"Yes, that's right , Tan," everybody would say each time, no matter how many repeats he gave.

It was the sort of thing that was encouraged by the lovely, enthusiastic warden Linda, who always joined in the fun, especially the finale of sing-along numbers that were probably written long before she was born but were sung lustily by all (well, nearly all) the residents.

The Valentine show covered a great distance as well as several years as far as I was involved. What do I remember best? Jimmy Skene, in serious mood playing some wonderful melodies and the same Jimmy Skene in skittish mood, either leaping up during Monti's 'Czardas' or down on one knee serenading some dear old lady, utterly bemused as he sang (?) his way through "'You Made Me Love You' in broadest Gallic.

David himself, taking both hands of some delighted female, going through the motions of a waltz or fox-trot which he crooned: "Are you lonesome tonight?" or, "When I fall in love."

And when she was able to tear herself away from work, Miriam delighting so many people with songs they knew and loved, David himself describing her as 'The Voice'.

They were happy days indeed with David and his Valentine Show, bringing a bit of sunshine and laughter into the lives of many who, otherwise might simply sit around all day just to meditate or brood in what someone, jokingly called 'the departure lounge'.

It was all so very worth while.

CHAPTER TWELVE

Take Your Partners

"**M**AY I have this dance please?" or more elegantly: "May I have the pleasure of this dance, please?" Phrases of a world that has gone, when everyone dressed in their elegant best, when the bands and orchestras played melodious tunes and couples had learned to dance the quick-step, fox-trot and waltz. In short, it was a time when there was that indefinable thing called style. The days of ballroom dancing, tea dances and the like are like the dodo. Or are they?

Well, not completely it seems. Even though the years have flown, leaving only the memories of my once famous Rémon Quartet that played all over the length and breadth of East Anglia when style was king, the enquiries for a 'proper band' to play for 'real dancing' have reached me by letter or telephone.

Of course, the Rémon Quartet is no more, Jack Wilkinson having died many years ago, Dick Pearce, following my rural escape, later having rusticated to Hevingham, and Dennis Payne in and out of so many combos, generally of the jazz genre.

A band can easily be brought together to play 'standards' for dancing, with many musicians like me, able to pick up the telephone, give the details of date, place, time, dress and most importantly, pay. In a matter of minutes you have a 'scratch' band, but one of great talent, for such is the strength of the friendship and reliance among the musical fraternity that you know the end product will be just right.

Top of the list for 'front' men was the everlasting Ivan Tooes, a sax/clarinet man who never let any tune beat him, despite his inability to read music but having a breath-taking musical dexterity. Ivan, who was a school pupil of my father's at the George White School in Norwich, played with just about every musician in Norfolk but not at the same time you will understand. Close behind Ivan would be another wizard of the clarinet, Peter Oxborough, though a somewhat difficult man to pin down, since he flitted from county to county with many bands, together with sorties to London too.

I managed to secure his services when I formed a four-piece for the silver wedding of my dear friends Robert and Vivien Laurie at the Barton Angler Hotel at Barton Turf in October 1998. Robert, a very keen jazz fan, had asked if I could get Peter to play, together with John Winsworth (bass) and Joe Jenkins (drums). We made a fair old sound in styles which ranged from trad jazz to Benny Goodman swing. Robert and Vivien were delighted with a most happy evening being had by all, as they say, and there was talk of the 'same again' for their pearl.

Peter again came with me, and John Winsworth too, to play at a memorable jazz day at The Swan Hotel, Southwold, as part of an Arts' Week there. I took two keyboards that day: Roland as straight piano and the Technics to provide vibes or guitar contribution and although we had no drums, the Benny Goodman/Artie Shaw sound was very good with a highly appreciative and knowledgeable audience.

It called to mind the time when the first seeds of interest in jazz had been sown for me.

In my first book *S'Wonderful*, I wrote of the jazz trio that entertained the boys at Norwich School during 'break' but could not recall the name of the pianist. Through the *Old Norvicensian* school magazine it has been revealed that he was David Cole, one of three brothers who has had an illustrious music career which included playing piano with the Royal Navy dance band at Weatherby in Yorkshire.

What talent came out of Norwich School! Bass players? Well, if I couldn't get John Winsworth, then I'd go for Dennis Payne or Brian Harvey (another from Norwich School), both of them highly-skilled men.

They used to say drummers were ten a penny but in my experience the really good ones come much dearer than that. The anonymous cruel and black joke used to refer to a bunch of musicians, plus a drummer, the inference being that the man on percussion wasn't classed as a musician. All you can say to that is: try playing for three or four hours without one to see how much you miss him.

In those days of early retirement I would, of course, have picked Dick Pearce but he was running a video shop (though he did tell me that when business was bad, he was actually running it down!) and worked until late, finding it impossible to do an evening gig.

Occasionally, Don Brewer and his mountainous drum kit would leave his other bands and join me, or there was the ever-faithful, willing and very able Rex Cooper, who was probably born with a pair of drumsticks in his hands, which I think are still attached.

However, the man I quickly fastened on to was the amiable Joe Jenkins, an ex-Londoner living in Brundall, who had gigged with all and sundry (that well-known theatrical pair!).

At weddings, it seemed that 'proper' music was wanted which I suppose might please the 'senior' guests and, by contrast, make the 'juniors' pull funny faces.

When Mr John Olorenshaw married for the second time, his reception was held at his home under a large marquee where I provided a quartet to play through the meal with dancing to follow. Dick Pearce got his drums out of the loft or garage (or was it hock?), John played bass guitar and Ivan blew up front, altogether making a good sound. Dick seemed to enjoy himself after such a long absence from the music scene and after remembering what went where and what hit this and that, settled down as if he'd only been on a week's holiday.

The most amusing thing about that gig was when a very well spoken gentleman came up to us and asked:

"How often do you practise together?"

I hadn't the heart to tell him, though John did murmur to me quietly: "We tend to practise separately."

To this day I'm not sure whether the questioner considered we were very good, clearly practising together a great deal, or that we were so awful as to be in need of a lot more. That I shall never know, but it did give rise to some quirky jocularity found among musicians, following his question.

Scottish wedding receptions obviously require Scottish music in the programme so when Rob Stevens' daughter Tiffany got wed I took Joe Dade along on accordion and included Jimmy Skene and Joe Jenkins. Tiffany had asked Miriam to sing, not necessarily Scottish songs, all of which went down well and later we were given a sumptuous supper in Rob's farmhouse there in Southrepps.

I felt it was a highly successful performance all round, an evening marred only by Miriam eating something which disagreed with her, leaving her quite ill for a couple of days.

At another Scottish wedding reception at Blofield Heath, I had booked Joe Dade, Joe Jenkins and John Winsworth, but when John called off I rang Ivan Tooes, always willing to give anything a try, who agreed to come. I made him a tape of reels and so on which he listened to and thoroughly mastered, like the excellent musician he is.

Unfortunately, I became quite ill just prior to the wedding, a persistent deep-seated cough leading to breathing problems which should have told me to cancel the job.

"The show must go on," they used to say and against my better judgement, as well as everyone else's, I went to lead my gallant band into action, throwing myself into 'The Dashing White Sergeant' and 'Eightsome Reel' with every fibre of my being. Well, not quite that …

Truth to tell, I struggled until the tape recorder took over, Miriam and the others carried the keyboard and amplification to the car and me with it. I was just able to hold out a feeble hand to pay the musicians. As for Ivan that night, he was superb and you would have thought he'd been playing reels all his life, so good was he. In fact, some of the guests thought he hailed from over the border and why was he not wearing his kilt?

The boys in the band as well as Miriam had been extremely worried about me, which they were certainly justified in so doing for it turned out that I had double pneumonia (never one to do things by halves) and had to go to bed for some time.

Surprise birthday parties are always good fun and when an old friend, Neville Reason, arranged one for his brother at Halesworth Town Hall in 1996, he asked me to get a band together.

I duly obliged, asking Ivan Tooes, John Winsworth and Joe Jenkins, as well as having Miriam to sing some suitable numbers.

When Neville's brother came into the hall, true to the tradition of these surprises, he couldn't believe it, such was the impact. A most enjoyable evening of music and dancing followed with Miriam singing, later joined by Neville himself, no mean jazz singer.

As I sat there playing, my mind went back to a gig we did there with the Rémon Quartet when we witnessed some unfortunate young man pitched over the balcony, though I hastily add that it was not a general feature of our gig world and I don't think the young man broke anything serious. A similar surprise took place at The Rookery, Fundenhall, the beautiful home of Mr Phil Sheridan, former Norwich Union executive and member of the Norfolk and Norwich Caledonian Society. The arrival of dozens of cars carrying guests was no birthday surprise: that was to come later.

As we, the now familiar Scottish band of Joe Jenkins, Joe Dade, John Winsworth and I, played quietly as people gathered with drinks and canapés on the sunlit terrace, I realised why the house was so named. From the woods just beyond Mr Sheridan's lawns came a continuous deafening caw of rooks, the like of which I have never encountered before, not only drowning conversation but the music too.

Joe tried a thunderous whack on his snare drum but to no avail, as the rooks seemed to turn up the volume as if in defiance.

The surprise was soon to come, the gift to Phil from his wife. Down the gravel drive and round on to the terrace marched twelve Scottish pipers, their music filling the air. Yes, twelve with the volume on maximum. Mr

Sheridan's face was a picture, something that clearly delighted his wife and his family as he watched the fully-uniformed brigade come to a halt to give us 'Scotland the Brave'. As they finished, everyone broke into loud applause. To the amazement of the lads and me, the rooks were silent. When it came to bagpipes it seemed, there was no contest!

The folk who frequented Wensum Lodge in Norwich, having a musical or rhythmic urge, together with a nostalgic look at times past, decided to hold a Sunday Tea Dance. Who should they ask to provide the music? One couple who knew me were Jim and Jean Newby and they telephoned to enquire if I could do it. Of course, being a Sunday I was booked regularly at the Oaklands, but decided I could manage the four o'clock start they had in mind and, since in those days we had two cars, Miriam would collect Jimmy Skene, rendez-vousing at Wensum Lodge.

Miriam, for her part, contributed some songs in between dances which were highly appreciated by a fairly large number of people. Quicksteps, fox-trots, waltzes and the occasional novelty dance kept the dancers busy until the break for tea. Well it would be tea, being a Tea Dance, wouldn't it? Tea and sandwiches, followed by cakes, provided the welcome refreshment, all of which found favour with Jimmy who used to declare that the food was the only reason he came along.

Jimmy himself was again the subject of great curiosity, both from his somewhat ancient look but more from his incredible violin dexterity and the apparent ease of his performance, the hall-mark of the professional.

It seemed that the Tea Dance had been a success, duly recorded with praise in the Wensum Lodge Gazette, or whatever they called their newspaper. A second one was arranged at a later date with both Jimmy and Miriam performing again and once more it was well attended.

The third and last one was not, which may have been due to the bad weather, illness or just bad publicity, but for whatever reason it meant no more, and the clink of tea cups together with our dulcet tones would not be heard at Wensum Lodge Palais de Danse again.

Playing solo for dancing is never easy and I suppose the only satisfactory way it can done is on the electronic organ, having considerable power and a multitude of sounds. I've done it a couple of times with the keyboard. The first was at a supper dance arranged for a Cavell School re-union when Don Hoffmann asked me to play, and Miriam, herself an ex-Cavell School girl, to sing. It was held at 'The Norfolk Dumpling' and although everyone declared it a success, I certainly missed a bass player and even more, a drummer.

The second time was at the Caledonian Society's President's supper dance and barbecue at Hempnall Village Hall when David Heighton had asked me to make the music on my own with his cashflow being a little sluggish I suspect. Anyway, I did it and together with Miriam's vocal contributions it seemed a successful venture, though I still missed the driving force of John on bass or violin and Joe on the drums. The 'voices" on the keyboard of bagpipes and accordion certainly helped to give an impression of authenticity about the overall sound.

In 1996 I had a call from my agent and friend Pat Few of Broadland Entertainments who said that the guests at the Hotel Nelson in Norwich wanted a 'little dance' at the end of their Christmas stay. They wanted – you've guessed it – 'proper dance music' from a 'proper band' and could the management arrange it, please?

The question came down the line to me, asking if I could bring a trio to the Nelson on the 27th of December. Now truth to tell, I rarely worked at Christmas (as a musician, that is), since I always believed it to be a family time and in my first full year of marriage to Miriam considered it a bit unfair.

However, these lofty thoughts were put aside when Pat mentioned the most lucrative of fees involved, which was why I accepted the gig and forsook the family fold, carefully mentioning that the money might help defray some of the festive outlay.

A trio? Well, it just had to be me, bass and drums, so without further ado I booked John Winsworth on bass and on drums a man highly regarded and revered among any percussion fraternity – Angus Honeyman.

Angus was 'Mr Percussion' to the County Education service, having taught dozens of rhythmic youngsters how to play tuned and untuned percussion instruments – properly, that is. Did he play dance music? Very much so and indeed I had joined him on one occasion at Brundall Globe to dep for his pianist John, which proved a most enjoyable if slightly noisy evening.

So there it was: my proper trio all set to play at the Nelson, the guests there eagerly awaiting the 27th of December.

Then came that awful telephone call, one which I shall always remember.

"Mr Tony Ireland?"

"Speaking."

"This is Kate Honeyman, Angus's daughter. My daddy died this morning."

It was like a body blow to me and I could only offer my inadequate words of condolence to a tearful Kate.

Some time later I attended the memorial service to Angus at St Peter Mancroft church where a huge number of musicians and others paid their tribute to a man who for me had been legendary in the music world. The eulogy by Ian Terry was absolutely superb, painting a picture of the man as we all knew him.

With just days to go to the Nelson engagement, I telephoned the ever-willing Rex Cooper who agreed to fill the drum spot.

On the night, the manager brought a bag full of 'spot' prizes to use up during the evening and John, Rex and I set off with quicksteps, foxtrots and waltzes, with a bit of Latin and novelty thrown in. We were in the Cannon bar and the people, mainly from greater London and Essex, danced happily around just as people used to, dancing contentedly, enjoying the old 'standards' and winning the odd prize.

Out came all the old chestnuts that I'd used so many times in the past:

"The first couple to bring me a picture of the Queen."

"Any man wearing a rose coloured shirt winds a prize."

or: "The prize goes to the first couple to bring me a set of back teeth."

All great fun.

My medleys of the dance tunes came one after the other with only a modulation between numbers to indicate a key change. John, on the bass, who speaks highly of the wealth of tunes that are all in my head, was quite brilliant at following me, changing key at a trice to be with me for the next number. As for Rex on the drums, change of key didn't seem to bother him but tempo was all important and his was impeccable.

The thanks we received at the end told us how successful the evening had been. Would we be there next year?

One gentleman, widower Charles Lock, was a friend of Vi Shaves, the former duettist with husband Ernie in my group Tony and Friends and told her what a great dancing night he'd enjoyed, the perfect end to his Christmas. Well, would we be there next year, they asked. We were, with the same formula and the same smiling enthusiasm from the hotel guests, albeit this time fewer in number. "Proper music" and "real dancing" it seemed were not quite dead. Perhaps in years to come both will be re-discovered and enjoy a revival. Who knows? One thing's for sure, though: my trio won't be around to tell.

CHAPTER THIRTEEN

You Ought To Be In Pictures

T*HE Cabinet of Doctor Caligari*, a very early horror film, was the first stepping stone in my haphazard career as a pianist for the 'silent cinema'.

At college, my great friend David Williams, secretary of the college film society, had persuaded me to provide the piano music for the film he had hired from The National Film Theatre. The success of my performance may have swelled my head into thinking that a career lay ahead for me, though these days there doesn't seem to be too many openings for cinema pianists. I wouldn't have thought that 'silent cinema pianist' would have much impact on a curriculum vitae in the area of job application. It would be about as useful as anyone claiming to be qualified in servicing incandescent gas mantles or bathing machines. So it was that my aspirations in that field came to naught until some forty years later when David Cleveland, film archivist of the University of East Anglia, got in touch with me.

"I'm having a show of East Anglian films at Cinema City, some of which are silent and need piano music," he said.   "Can you – and will you do it?"

I told him I would be delighted, and duly went along to Cinema City where I met both David Cleveland and the proprietor of the cinema, Kingsley Canham, both most charming gentlemen.

David showed me to the great German upright piano situated half-way down the left aisle and set at an angle so that I could see the screen and also David. He introduced the films which he preceded by introducing me to the audience, indicating that some of the films had me as 'the soundtrack'.

It was a nostalgic look at scenes of towns and villages, of farming, shooting and flying, from an age long past to which I added my snippets of music to each one. If there were an old seaside scene for example, I strummed a few bars of 'I do like to be beside the seaside' and 'Those magnificent men in their flying machines' for an air display, somewhat corny I suppose but it did give some amusement to members of the audience.

135

Both David and Kingsley were delighted, asking me if I would consider further shows to which I was pleased to agree to do.

I have to say that I gave the German piano, by G Schwechten, ten out of ten, for it was a real beauty, clearly looked after and tuned regularly with the powerful bass so prevalent as in all German makes. It made playing a joy and I could hardly wait to get back.

That soon came when David Cleveland put on a programme entitled *Ration Days* which, as the name suggests, was a series of shorts about the austerity of wartime and how people coped. Early in the show, King's Lynn Home Guard were featured where I strummed bars of 'Who do you think you are kidding, Mr Hitler?', 'This is the army Mr Jones' and 'Praise the Lord and pass the ammunition'.

A short colour film showed bombed Norwich where I added 'Home sweet home' and minor key phrases when graves were featured. With the American airfields pictured I put in bars of 'American Patrol' which on piano sounded a little limp, remembering the Glenn Miller version, 'Over There' and 'A Wing and a Prayer'.

From a news-reel came footage of a pre-fab being lowered into place in Norwich with the family then moving in to which I added 'This old house' and when the mother kissed her daughter, 'Goodnight sweetheart'.

Sometimes songs or tunes are so easy to associate with the film such as when the 1948 cricket match at Southend against the Australians was shown I played 'Tie me kangaroo down ', and for the Fen farming clips 'We plough the fields and scatter' closely followed by 'The Archers' were obvious choices.

David Cleveland's archive film shows were (and still are) very popular, not only at the 'home base' of Cinema City but when on tour round the county. When I have been unavailable, David has called upon the very capable Barry Bryant or Roger Cooke, both able to play without the encumbrance of music, but just looking at the screen. I suppose you might (with that old musician's sense of humour) call it 'playing at sight'.

One of the archive productions was the *Broads Shows* which to East Anglians would convey pictures of open stretches of water though to an American something entirely different.

David's Norfolk version in 1999 appeared at Norwich's Assembly House, Great Yarmouth, Beccles, Loddon, Stalham and Wroxham, the last-named being where I came in at the village hall on a Saturday night in November. I could hardly believe it when I saw huge numbers of people queuing to get in for this cinema celebration of the Broads that I could only wonder at their eager enthusiasm or cynically imagine that they had peeped to see what was the usual trash on Saturday night's television.

As it was, the hall was pronounced full by 7.45pm with more than eighty people turned away. In fact I was fortunate that no one had pinched my seat at the piano. David Cleveland introduced the evening with a brief account of the films on show, pointing out that the silent clips would be accompanied by piano music provided by Mr Tony Ireland.

Slides, rather than moving film, began the show with stills from the late 19th century to which I played all manner of appropriate tunes to do with water. During the course of that evening I put in snippets of many watery songs and tunes including 'Lazy River', 'Sailing', 'Messing about on the River', 'Red Sails in the Sunset', to say nothing of classics like Handel's 'Water Music' and Saint-Saens' 'The Swan'. The show was a huge triumph for David who received great applause, just as I did when he proffered his thanks to me for the accompaniment.

When the directors at Woodbridge's Riverside Theatre contacted me in 1995 to play for the silent film section of their 80th birthday celebrations, I felt highly honoured. Miriam and I travelled down to Woodbridge where we parked by the theatre, which had formerly been known as the Woodbridge Electric Theatre. Inside, we met Stuart Saunders, Stephen Peart and projectionist Paddy O'Brian Baker and we were made very welcome. Miriam sat in the auditorium while I seated myself at the big grand piano, just below the screen to be given a preview of the four films for which I was to play.

Cupid's Entanglement with Alan Hale was a melodramatic pastiche where love conquers all, after which we had *Love, Speed and Thrills* with crazy and frenetic Keystone Kops, ever involved in chases and trick effects. Next was *Sweedie Learns to Swim*, a comic caper with the ugliest of men, Wallace Beery who once declared, "My ugly mug has been my fortune."

My part of the evening's programme ended with Charlie Chaplin in *His Night Out*, a typical round of mistakes, twitchings and banana skin slips straight out of the Chaplin book of comedy. Chaplin once said: "All I need to make a comedy is a park, a policeman and a pretty girl."

After an informative talk given by Stuart Saunders about the Woodbridge Theatre, there followed a playlet given by the Deben Players entitled *Electric*.

The silent films were introduced and I was soon letting my fingers loose on the piano, filling in the bits for gaiety or sadness, quiet or noisy, calm or frantic, as well as the split second timed moments of a slide, a drop, a kick or a smack. The films were quite long really, the Chaplin being a two-reeler, at times somewhat tedious, which made it the hardest of the four to accompany. However, it was all deemed to be a great success with splendid round of applause at the end with my name linked to it, something which tends to give you a tingle and think it was worth the effort. Certainly the glowing letter of praise with thanks I received some days later indicated as much.

In 2001, I was asked by Richard Young of Little Ellingham if I would play for his show of silent films in July. He had already approached a younger pianist who said he would have to locate the music in public libraries, all of which would take time – time that Mr Young did not have. When I said the whole thing could be done without music, Richard Young booked me there and then, promising to let me have the list of films and their synopses.

There were seven films, six of them quite short with the main feature *Drama on the Matterhorn* lasting forty minutes. This was a German reel made in 1928, involving love and treachery with much of the action set on the high peaks of one of Switzerland's most famous mountains. It clearly called for highly dramatic music with minor chords but softer bits for the romantic scenes. Anyway, with a programme of music I had put together for the films, I arrived at Berry Hall, Little Ellingham, where Richard Young lived. It was a beautiful summer evening and Richard and his wife welcomed me in where I had a glass of wine before being shown the 'cinema'. This was reminiscent of Peter Sellers' *Smallest Show on Earth*, being the upstair part of a converted barn having a screen at one end with seating for about thirty or so people. I set up my Technics keyboard at one side, diagonally facing the screen so as to have a clear view.

The audience duly arrived, making their way up an outside staircase to seat themselves on plastic chairs and await the performance. After a brief introduction from Richard in which he included a mention of the pianist, the show began.

The shorts included one from the *Our Gang* series, children's comedies produced in the 1920s, this one entitled *Full Steam Ahead*. In it I used train songs like 'The Runaway Train' and 'Chattanooga Choo Choo' with just a snippet of Vivian Ellis's 'Coronation Scot'.

There was *Air Highways* with a flight in the Graf Zeppelin from Germany to Gibraltar, a clip from *Flying Down to Rio* (1930) and a bi-plane trip across the Andes. The scope for music here was great: 'Up and Away', 'Fly Me to the Moon' and naturally 'Those magnificent Men in Their Flying Machines'.

Take the Air was slapstick humour on a building site and *Beanstalk Mickey* was Disney's Mickey Mouse as Jack in *Jack and the Beanstalk* with my contribution of Charles Williams' 'Devil's Galop' (The Dick Barton music) in the final chase scene. It was altogether a most pleasant evening, with interesting chats afterwards with some of the audience who told me of their own memories of early cinema.

At Cinema City in 1999 I had to play for a most bizarre 1923 film from Germany called *Mysteries of a Hairdresser's Shop* with a script by Bertolde Brecht, a sort of Sweeney Todd blood and thunder. In it, beheaded bodies moved around, as well as severed body parts, including heads which I think is known as Surrealist art form, so naturally I played what I thought was surrealist music.

In April 2000, the East Anglian Archives at the University of East Anglia led by the enthusiastic David Cleveland held their 25th Anniversary at Cinema City on Wednesday the 25th. Whilst the many invited guests arrived for drinks, I played appropriate music on the lovely German upright, stopping only for brief words with those visitors who recognized me.

On the Saturday following, the 28th, I played there for *A Century of Films*, a programme devised by the Archive Group lasting two hours, though not all piano! This show, which was part of the Silver Anniversary was a sell-out with many civic dignitaries present.

The programme opened with a rare piece of footage from 1909 of Norwich people 'going to an event', followed by a 1905 Hepworth comedy *The Fatal Sneeze*. Other silent shorts were *How Kippers leave Home*, shot at Lowestoft, *Southwold Railway 1929*, *Mistley Coronation Celebration* and *Stiffkey Marshes in the cold winter of 1963,* which were easy enough to play for, albeit not over inspiring.

Can you imagine Shakespeare plays without sound? It seems anachronistic, rather like having a ventriloquist on radio, although in fact was done by Peter Brough with his dummy Archie Andrews, as well I remember. Would an audience come to watch plays by the Bard performed in silence?

I recall a gentleman filling the Royal Festival Hall in London to capacity where he gave a piano recital on an instrument that had had the internal workings removed. A hushed and enraptured audience watched as he played with scintillating flourishes various masterly works, full of arpeggios, powerful chords, diatonic and chromatic runs with glissandos sprinkled all over the place. He finished to tumultuous applause, a standing ovation which may or may not have something to say about British music appreciation.

Actually, dear old Joseph Cooper used to do the same thing on the 'dummy keyboard' every week in his spot on *Face the Music* as part of a quiz where the panel had to guess what he was playing. Robin Ray, a fount of knowledge on classical music, would know it from the first bar, invariably.

So, if you can get people to pay money to listen to a silent piano, could you get them to watch *Silent Shakespeare*, for that was how Kingsley Canham billed it at Cinema City. I was designated to play the piano accompaniment, though I hasten to say, not silent piano. It did attract the crowds who poured in to see it, Miriam my chief critic among them.

There were three films. The first, *King John*, was what remained of a four-scene film made in 1899 to be discovered in archives in the Netherlands in such a poor state that only one scene remained. This was a mere three and a half minutes of one of the earliest movies directed by W K L Dixon for the

British Mutascope and Biograph Company with Herbert Beerbohm-Tree in the title role. The scene depicted the death of the king, which meant much of my playing was in the minor key.

There followed two full-length Shakespearian tragedies, both made in Denmark in the 1920s, the first being *Othello* with Emil Jannings in the title role. Again, as with *King John* the music had to be in tragic style mainly in the minor keys.

Mercifully there was an interval between that and the next film *Hamlet* with Asta Nielsen as the Prince of Denmark. Once more, death stalked the screen with no let up in the misery – in fact 'nothing to laugh at , at all'. Actually, there were so many killings, deaths and funerals on the screen that evening I began to think that by the end I would be joining them. That I couldn't be, since I had been billed as 'live piano accompaniment', although I did point out to a patron that not ever having seen the films before, I had gone into the programme 'cold'.

When *Hamlet* drew to its close at around 11pm there came an unusual and somewhat bizarre denouement in which the dying lead, Asta Nielsen, was revealed as a woman. I personally never considered that Hamlet might have been a woman, but since it was a Danish production about a prince of Denmark, then I expect they know more about such things and wouldn't argue with that, bowing to their superior knowledge.

When these film shows end and the lights go up, a great many interesting people come and talk to me, telling me of fathers, grandfathers and aunts who played the piano for the early movies. One elderly lady told me how she remembered her father playing surrounded by a strong wire cage to protect him from the cinema hooligans who would pelt him with all kinds of missiles at a performance. Thankfully, I never had to endure such things.

In my career as pianist for the silent cinema I have been expertly guided by my great friend David Williams, whose knowledge of the moving picture industry must be second to none, a veritable walking encyclopaedia on the subject.

For a performance of two Buster Keaton films, David sent me a video of both of them, thus enabling Barry Bryant and me, who shared the piano duties, to see them in advance which most certainly helped.

My good friends David Cleveland and Kingsley Canham always showed me the utmost kindness and courtesy and always proffered thanks and praise along the way and I have found the whole exercise so fascinating and absorbing to make myself almost part of the screen action as I wander the keys.

And they said that when the Talkies came, the likes of me would be out of a job...

CHAPTER FOURTEEN

There's No Business Like Show Business

" S PIXWORTH Variety Group are putting on a pantomime." "Oh no they're not." "Oh yes they are .... If they can get a pianist, that is.

So what did they do? Like a lot of other companies they appealed to Derek James in the Eastern Evening News, who tender hearted as he is, relayed their problem in his nightly column.

There it was for all to read: "Anyone who can help, please contact Elizabeth Moy at Spixworth."

Now I have to say that pantomimes are not, as they say, my scene, never having liked them from childhood, finding them rather silly with a good excuse for some awful pop singer to inflict his or her 'latest single' on a captive audience. Originally, as I am given to understand, pantomimes were plays in mime as the second part of the word implies and I felt then (and still do) they might be better performed thus.

However, I may have fancied myself as a pianist in bright shining armour as it were and like a modern Sir Galahad offered my help to Mrs Moy. It was a tight schedule with little time to rehearse which had the additional snag of my not being able to be there for two of the performances.

Elizabeth Moy, who was quite charming, introduced me to the cast, Mike Alden the author of the pantomime and also comic dame, Steve Bullock, the general factotum of the whole thing and the ancient piano which was to be the 'orchestra' for each show. I would have given it less than six out of ten since it was certainly in need of a good piano doctor.

Who did I know could fill the two performances which I couldn't make? Not an easy matter with good pianists in short supply. Before I had joined Madge Mildinhall's Singing Seniors, they had had Brenda Binns playing for them, a highly-respected pianist from Taverham whose husband Chris was in the catering business.

Brenda agreed to come along to a rehearsal at Spixworth where she watched and made notes (no pun intended) and accepted the request to share music duties with me. And so it was that between us we provided the music for the Spixworth pantomime that Christmas in 1990.

Was it a success?

Oh no it wasn't!

Oh yes it was!

Indeed it was, with a full house at every show: grannies, uncles, aunts and cousins – all there to support the village effort and laugh and clap in all the right places – well most of the time anyway.

For the warmer part of the next year the Spixworth group put on *Showtime '91*, a variety show featuring songs and sketches with music and dances from the members with a finale of 'The Good Old Days', Edwardian music hall. I had been asked to act as accompanist and in her notes in the programme Elizabeth Moy wrote: "Since last December we have had the good fortune to have the incomparable Tony Ireland play the piano for us as a result of our plea in the *Eastern Evening News*. He is totally unflappable and does whatever we ask of him, offering advice where necessary. Without him this show would not have been the same."

Praise indeed, though I had never thought of myself as unflappable, as my wife Miriam could well testify.

When the audience added their contributions to the 'Good Old Days' it took my mind back to those college nights at Tooting 'Castle', part of my Salad days of so many songs of a long time ago. It was all very enjoyable and since they were all so enthusiastic and friendly, I readily agreed to be 'Mr Music' for *Sinbad*, their next pantomime, again written by Mike Alden playing the dame once more.

My rôle continued for the next two years with *Snow White and the Seven Dwarfs* and *Cinderella*, the formula hardly varying but technical effects becoming more and more inventive and put to use. When it came to *Puss in Boots* the following year, I introduced the company to Jimmy Skene, my highly-talented violinist friend. Derek James did a good article about it for the *Eastern Evening News* in which Jimmy, then 82 declared: "Tony and the music have brought me back to life."

Of course, when the young members of the Spixworth Variety Group set eyes on Jimmy, there was much amused giggling, for he did have a wrinkled walnut appearance with a head that was mainly bald, giving a hint of veracity to his press statement. I suppose a little mickey-taking was inevitable but, when Jimmy started to play his violin, the giggles evaporated and were replaced by awesome looks on the young faces, who were now totally speechless. His playing was like nothing they had ever experienced for talent like his was unknown in their world of tinsel pop and plastic ephemera.

In *Cinderella* in 1994, again written by Mike Alden, the now archetypal dame, there were further effects of strobe lighting and such that produced 'oohs' and 'aahs' from the audience which contributed to another Spixworth success. Miriam came along to see that particular one and was made most welcome by Elizabeth Moy and her colleagues. They were a most enterprising company, full of youthful vigour with lots of ideas and I was privileged to work with them.

Our trio of Jimmy Skene, Joe Dade and I entertained at Catton Court in Old Catton, Norwich, for a party where Celia, the warden had booked us, though how she ever knew of us is lost in the mists of time, as they say. What I do remember is that we were well received and well wined and dined, something which always pleased Joe and Jimmy, undoubtedly improving their playing immensely.

The piano in the communal lounge was a good one, the property of a resident, Mr John Watson, an ex-naval man whose two sons had been at Thorpe Hamlet school during my time there as teacher. With such a good instrument, and the likes of Jimmy and Joe behind me, the music fairly breezed along, making the evening go with a swing.

Such was the success of it all that Celia asked us to play at the Christmas party there, when I took along a fine clarinet friend Geoff Haworth. Again we were royally treated. Each of us receiving a wrapped gift from them, as I recall simulating the shape of a bottle.

Now among the residents was a lady called Joan Green, who it seemed had been involved in 'show business' in a semi-pro way most of her life and approached us to see if we would be interested in furthering her erstwhile career. Joan, a Londoner, was married to Bob, who had served in Bomber Command during the war. When war ended Bob became a teacher, later being promoted to head of a school in Leigh-on-Sea in Essex. On retirement, the couple moved to Halesworth in Suffolk where Bob had a stroke, forcing them to find sheltered accommodation in old Catton in Norwich.

Joan, determined to carry on entertaining, decided that the folk of Catton needed livening up with a show or two, which is where we came in. She recruited from among the ranks, finding singers, dancers, comedians and scene painters. Among the cast I remember husband and wife, Ray and Moira Unwin, impressionist and extrovert Eric Winter, Carol Weir, a competent song and dance girl, and John Bray, the retired policeman who could paint scenery like John Constable (no pun intended). Then there was Joe Dickerson with a grin from ear to ear and an almost permanent infectious laugh, who could transform himself into all kinds of characters. He used to do a very funny rendition of 'If I Could Plant a Tiny Seed of Love' in the style of a wet simpleton.

The dynamic Joan led all this lot, making costumes, organizing the running order, writing the script and even adding her own song contributions or duets. She left the musical direction to me and a show was born. They filled Old Catton Village Hall, old and young alike (though mostly old) who roared at the antics on stage and bellowed out the chorus finale, leaving everyone happy and wondering why it all seemed so much better than television.

Joan wondered if we could do another, making it Olde Tyme Music Hall and asked me to come up with some ideas when I met her for coffee in Jarrold's to discuss matters.

That show came to fruition, one of the highlights being John, the policeman, dressed as the bride in 'Waiting at the Church', totally grotesque and of course immediately recognized by the entire audience. Joan pulled in my great friend Royle Drew to join the cast, his best-loved contribution being 'Nobody Loves a Fairy When She's Forty', a bizarre figure in tights and tutu.

The show's success became a precedent for others to follow with a regular rendez-vous with Joan and me at Jarrold's to discuss the content and format of the programme. Christmas shows and summer shows followed in succession filled with Joan's clever ideas with songs and dances, sketches and audience participation.

I remember that the hall had an altercation with a nearby resident who said she could hear the piano in her home, situated as it was stage right (the piano, not her home). It was decided to placate the lady by moving the piano to stage left which meant, of course that once moved to that position, it could not be shifted elsewhere, somewhat restricting stage direction.

In one of Joan Green's concerts she included scenes and songs from *The Wizard of Oz* and persuaded my daughter Elisabeth to play Dorothy, who I must say gave a fine rendition of 'Over the Rainbow'. On that occasion, Joan's daughter Diana was present and was able to witness the success of her mother's efforts. A mini version of the show was performed at Catton Court as well as at St Paul's Church Hall, Hellesdon, for the elderly folk there.

The greatest triumph for Joan was her last show, packed full of patriotic song, a miniature form of *Last Night of the Proms*, the stage awash with Union flags. Miriam, who had joined the cast, dressed in a long white robe came forward to sing 'Rule Britannia' with the audience giving their vocal addition to the chorus. The show reached a tremendous climax when Joe cried from the back of the hall: "Mafeking has been relieved!"

Loud cheering followed and Joan came forward to take her bows, along with the cast and the musicians.

Sadly, acute arthritis and the death of her husband Bob, forced Joan to quit her stage work but I'm certain there will be people in Old Catton who will remember her wonderful shows for a long time to come.

In 1997 I had a call from Sheila Moore of the Phoenix Performing Arts Group asking me to be MD for their production of *Gypsy*, the musical by Jule Styne and Stephen Sondheim. I accepted the challenge with rehearsals held in Bowthorpe village, directed by the energetic, enthusiastic Sheila.The songs were great with well-known numbers such as 'Let Me Entertain You', 'Wherever We Go' and 'Ev'rything's Coming Up Roses'. The stage craft was handled most sensitively by Sheila, for since it was the story of striptease artiste Gypsy Rose Lee, some near nudity was required. She herself took the rôle of Rose (Senior) appearing in the second half of the show.

The production was held at Earlham School, where I had the talented Danny Howard on drums for the first two nights and the equally gifted Keith Wickham on the third. It was a resounding success with good press reviews.

David Valentine, expressing his feelings about the show, wrote: "Special praise should be given to Sheila Moore who produced and directed it and her daughter Teresa, all the cast, stage crew and all concerned. Musical accompanists Tony and Danny were excellent."

Gypsy would be one of the last shows of its kind with a wealth of good songs to leave the audience humming them on their way home. I enjoyed every minute of the show, which had some great music and was so beautifully staged.

The Helm Players put on *Pinocchio* at Heartsease Methodist Church Hall where I played keyboard for them, even though it was a 'strange' keyboard, not mine. It was good production with special effects and one that played to a good house each night.

At Central Hall, Wymondham, a concert was arranged in aid of the Romanians. The first half included the Ad Hoc Entertainers and Jimmy and me with a tribute to Gershwin, with the second half devoted to the big band sound directed by Peter Fenn, former musical director of Anglia Television. It was a great night all round but I was stunned by Peter and his merry men – superb musicians all.

Finally, I have to tell you about a remarkable lady who Miriam and I met in 2001. She was Maureen Johnson, affectionately known as 'Nanny Johnson', since her professional career had been 'nanny' to dozens of children, mainly sons and daughters of the gentry.

By now she had retired, chiefly for health reasons, and had married David and set up a pram repair business at Carbrooke near Watton. Even out there in that remote countryside she would have regular visits or news from former 'babies' who it seemed had never forgotten her.

So how and why did she get in touch with Miriam and me?

The 'how' part was through Radio Norfolk when she discovered that we were in the business of entertainment. The 'why' question was quite fascinating.

Maureen and David have a love of the 'Forties, particularly the 1939–45 era, and decided to have a charity evening at Central Hall in Wymondham. Since Maureen's own health problems related to the heart, the proceeds were to go to the Heart Foundation, not surprisingly. She asked us to provide the ENSA bit, that which entertainers used to laughingly refer to as 'Every Night Something Awful', which was general entertainment for the armed services.

We put together a 'concert party' recruiting Royle Drew, Oz and Wendy Topliff to join Miriam with me as accompanist. Added to this, my daughter Elisabeth arranged with dancer friend Jenny Bugg to have a dance troupe to provide a lively tap routine of boys and girls from Norwich.

"I need a 'Forties dance band," said Nanny, "a big band in the Glenn Miller style would be too expensive. What do you suggest?"

I knew at once who would be just the man: my great friend, the indestructible Ivan Tooes, who knew just about every number in the 'A to Z' of popular song and could find a quartet of musical sages to give Nanny just what was needed.

Some of us met at Maureen's cottage, where amidst mounds of sandwiches, sausage rolls and cakes, we planned the evening. Her cottage was filled with 'Forties memorabilia, even to a *Daily Mirror* 'Wanted' poster for Adolf Hitler, which offered a substantial reward, dead or alive. There were photographs of Nanny's former houses with many of those who had been in her care, as well as numerous prams about, together with two very life-like babies that were more than dolls, since they bore the weight of real babies.

That charity evening was quite amazing with Chantry Hall filled with people all in period costume who had paid for dancing, entertainment and fish and chips supper, all of which the dynamic Maureen Johnson had organized. Ivan's band played 'Forties music, familiar to him and his three buskers: Rex Cooper on the drums, John Winsworth on double bass and Arthur Maton on keyboard.

In poured military personnel from the armed forces, including squadron leaders, majors, petty officers, WAAFs, WRACs, WRENs and even land-girls. Those ladies who were in civvies had actually drawn black lines down the back of their stockings!

Our ENSA group went on where Miriam, Oz and Wendy sang wartime songs and Royle performed (for the very first time) his Robb Wilton sketch – 'The Day War Broke Out', which went down so very well. The dancers did their tap routine superbly and then it was time for supper. Outside in the car park the fish and chip man had arrived, aptly called 'The Cod Father' and people queued in 'Forties fashion for their cod or plaice and chips.

Miriam described how weird it seemed to have dozens of people in wartime uniform all lined up at the chip van, making it seem like a time warp, the only difference being that lights were on everywhere which would not have been so during the war.

With supper ended, the band took over for dancing, which included a dance from the wartime called 'The Blackout Stroll', which, as the title indicates, was a dance to be done in the dark. Maureen had procured the music and the record, and had handed both to Ivan and the rest was easy – well, for him anyway.

It had been an incredible evening with over 200 people gathered together, all in costume, to re-live a time when most of them hadn't been born, in order to raise a lot of money for a worthy cause. The whole thing had been the brain child of Maureen 'Nanny' Johnson, something to which we felt privileged to contribute our own particular talents, for it was nostalgia at its best and Maureen is, as somebody said 'some special lady'.

CHAPTER FIFTEEN

A Tinkling Piano

"**Y**OU see, what we need is some nice background music during the meal." I wonder how many pianists have heard that, the familiar words of a secretary, chairman or president who wants what is known as 'wallpaper music', where the pianist, chameleon-like, blends in with the surroundings.

Notice, it has to be nice background music, not easy to define exactly but you do have an inkling of what they mean and he is paying the piper so he does call the tune – well, almost.

"What we don't want," continues the guv'nor, "is all that loud stuff. Do you know, my wife and I were at a wedding last month...."

And he goes on to tell you how the 'music' was so loud you couldn't have a normal conversation. It's all right: I've heard it all so many times, like so many other 'legit' musicians.

"It's all right sir. I play nice music quietly. You'll hardly notice me."

You can see the relief written all over him.

Hotel work is extremely enjoyable for the most part. I've watched countless old films where you see or hear the pianist in the lounge or restaurant providing that relaxed and sophisticated backdrop to the scene, just enough to hear him and recognize a melody or two. One of the joys of a 'cocktail' pianist is that you can play exactly what you like because, after all, you are only providing a sound to fill in the background as it were, where some will be heard, some half heard and the rest 'fall on stony ground'.

It reminds me of an organist friend of mine who maintained that very few members of the congregation actually took notice of what he played before service and to prove his point, one Sunday morning played his own arrangement of 'Yes, we have no bananas'.

Now whether it was because those who identified his recital dared not mention it or that his theory was totally vindicated, we shall never know but he sailed through 'Bananas' without a murmur.

When I joined a rota of organists at a Norwich church, I found the congregation extremely noisy before service with my musical contribution fairly drowned in the hubbub. Remembering my friend's 'success' with 'Yes, we have no bananas' I decided to try the same idea (though not the same song for I would hate to be accused of plagiarism), traversing the manuals with an interpretation of 'Rudolf the Red Nosed Reindeer'. Well, it was Christmas, after all.

Suffice to say that I think I was the only one who noticed it.

The icing on the cake for the solo pianist is to have a piano or at the very least one of the playable variety, by which I mean that a piano is in situ rather than having to cart your own.

At South Walsham Hall was the smallest grand piano I've ever seen, the property of the Swiss owner. It stood in the large lounge, mercifully well away from the huge log fire, but nevertheless required regular tuning which I suspect was due to its small size. Saturday night was 'live music', a misnomer really since I haven't come across dead music (except at funerals) and the 'live' part presumably refers to the performer, though having witnessed some on occasions, that fact might cast some doubt.

Piano duties in those days were shared in alternate weeks by Peter Williams and me and more latterly by Barry Bryant with my 'depping' when he was unavailable. In fact when I returned there after some six years of absence, the head waiter was still there and I said :

"Sergio, it's six years you know and you don't look any different."

"And you sir, are a very good liar," he replied.

Sadly, South Walsham Hall closed with Sergio apparently losing a lot of invested money. I had a soft spot for the hall and also Sergio, for it was he who, on the night that Miriam and I got engaged there, presented us with a half bottle of champagne and again one year later brought Miriam a corsage and presented our first drinks with compliments.

At 'The Pheasant' at Kelling they had a beautiful grand, near full size I believe which stood in the restaurant. The only snag about that one was that it stood on bare boards and the management's instructions to the dinner pianist was to 'play it quietly as the diners didn't like it too loud'. As an experienced pianist, I know that with the best will in the world, to play a huge grand, which is standing on a wooden floor, quietly, is a difficult thing and since the instrument in question had a heavy action anyway, it was far from easy. I found in the end it was simplest to depress both the loud and soft pedal together to obtain the 'acceptable' sound level.

They had a grand at The Oasis Hotel which I think was a Challen but nothing to write home about, though on my last visit there as a wedding guest it was a much better instrument, a Yamaha I believe.

The Chappell family (nothing to do with the English piano makers) kept Drayton Wood Hotel on the outskirts of Norwich and through agent Benny Lyon, booked me in 1989 to play there on New Year's Eve, in Norfolk known as 'Old Year's Night'.

Mr Chappell, a Greek Cypriot, hired a Kawai baby grand from Allen's of Great Yarmouth for the night which gave me the greatest joy to play. In the main it was dinner music but I did have to play for some dancing, rather in the way that in pre-war films people got up to dance at any point during supper.

Close to midnight Mr Chappell would connect a microphone next to a portable radio so that the midnight chimes of Big Ben could reverberate all round the hotel, whereupon I would play 'Auld Lang Syne' to a large circle of guests. It was a great night, particularly enjoyable for me on such a lovely piano, plus the fact that Mr Chappell, his wife and son Andrew, and all the staff were such charming people, showing me the utmost courtesy and presenting me with a bottle of champagne as a bonus gift.

It was therefore not too surprising that I was asked back the following year and although the second time can never match the first, it was enjoyable none the less with the same Kawai hired for me. I recall that on that particular night my daughter Elisabeth telephoned me at midnight, a waiter bringing the 'phone over to the piano when I spoke to her seconds after 'Auld Lang Syne' to wish her a happy new year and she to me.

For five consecutive New Year's Eves I played at Drayton Wood and although it was an enjoyable experience, by the end the customers were not the same and I think Mr Chappell Senior wasn't showing quite the same enthusiasm and possibly not quite the same profits. Shortly afterwards, the hotel was sold to become a Thai restaurant which after a short spell was transformed into a nursing home. Strange really, since before the Chappells bought it, it had been a nursing home for the elderly.

Other venues which had their own pianos were 'The Arlington', which later became 'The George' off Newmarket Road, and 'The Greens' near Aylsham where owner Brenda Binns kept her own upright. I played both (not simultaneously) with music merging into the background in customary fashion.

The title of this chapter, 'A Tinkling Piano' is a quote from the song 'These Foolish Things', composed in 1936 when I imagine the writers Eric Maschwitz (words) and Jack Strachey (music) would never have conceived that one day keyboards would be substitutes for pianos. In any case 'a tinkling keyboard in the next apartment' doesn't have quite the same ring, does it?

There was a time when almost every hotel, restaurant, bar and pub had its own piano which actually got played. Not any more. They took up room, had to be tuned and maintained and 'Musak' came along, cheaper than the average pianist with the result that pianos were sold off or consigned to a basement and pianists went through a spate of redundancy.

Hotels and restaurants had their piped music while bars and pubs installed the infernal juke box to oust the Joanna. Occasionally one was allowed to stay in a corner to be littered with glasses and bottles, something of a curiosity, a sad phenomenon endeavouring to stay upright and even look grand.

When both management and patrons tired of the monotonous drone of disembodied sounds filling their eating and drinking places, somebody hit on a great idea : 'live' music. In other words, bring back the real musicians, some from retirement, others presumably out of storage or even rigor mortis.

A few pianos still remained but most returning troubadours brought their own keyboards which not only produced the sound of a piano (even a grand) but all kinds of instruments from sax to trumpet, from clarinet to trombone, even a sitar. A sitar ? Yes, indeed – most useful for Divali.

Along with the all the others, I succumbed to a keyboard, first a Roland as I have mentioned and then a Technics, both Japanese masterpieces, the latter capable of anything, most of all making many musicians redundant.

In earlier gigs I was booked as 'Tony and Roland', carting along to two big Masonic dinner dances at Hotel Norwich where I played the supper music as well as the accompaniment for the Ladies' Song. I think the third time I went with Technics replacing Roland, they were quite disappointed, nay upset, and thought that he might be unwell.

Of course, Technics travels with me to The Oaklands where I tend to take a 'softly, softly' approach, playing just loud enough for patrons to hear me, yet able to hold a conversation. New friends, regulars to the hotel, joined the ranks of my fans, including Clifford and Val Burling, David and Daphne Abra, Bill and Queenie Kilbourn, Nigel and Audrey Emerson and Neville Nelson and his wife Viola (very musical!), Neville an ex-Avenue Road boy. Barbara Goldsmith and husband Eddie are very early arrivals there every week, Barbara having been a teaching colleague in former days, while Brian and Jo Loveday always sit and enjoy my music after lunch.

All of them help give me that warm and friendly feeling that makes The Oaklands a family affair, helped in no small way by the amiable and likeable management and staff.

My keyboard has been with me at Barnham Broom Country Club for weddings and at The Links Golfing Hotel at West Runton, not only for weddings but for several years' running on St Valentine's night where I have endeavoured to provide romantic sounds for romantic diners.

Technics came to the Jurnet Room at Wensum Lodge for a birthday celebration, to The Anchor Hotel at Walberswick where half a dozen people of 'a certain age' enjoyed my music and to 'The Swan' at Southwold where, on a snowy night, I played first upstairs and then down in the bar. On that particular occasion, New Year's Eve 1995, Miriam came with me and Dudley Clarke, the then manager was extremely kind and courteous to both of us, offering us refreshments and champagne. My booking was until 11pm after which we made tracks for home, hoping to arrive in time to see in the new year. Unfortunately, we drove straight into a snow drift, were spotted by a knight of the road in a 4 x 4 and towed out. As we drove gingerly the rest of the way, we heard the chimes of Big Ben on the car radio.

Rob and Judy Piercy invited me to their home at Ashwellthorpe, where I played lunchtime music in their large entrance hall, while dozens of people walked about with a plate and glass of wine, occasionally stopping to have a word with me. I met Rob and Judy again when they retired to Richmond Court in Cromer, but sadly when they decided to return to Wymondham, Rob died.

Occasionally, my keyboard wasn't needed, such as for private functions at the Norwich Assembly Rooms where in the Music Room sits a beautiful full-sized Steinway grand. It's great to play, once you've shown it who's master, for like many Steinways it has a heavy action and requires some attack.

At Boswell's , when I was 'live music', an upright stood on a small dais where I was accompanied by Brian Harvey on bass guitar to the further accompaniment of bottles and glasses. There we pounded out jazz as advertised and although I have to admit I am not strictly a jazz pianist, the customers seemed to enjoy it all enough for us to be offered return bookings.

On one such night I was to meet someone who would have a huge impact on my life. A party of American tourists were in Boswell's restaurant listening to our music and during our break, a lady introducing herself as Kathleen Bracken, got into deep conversation with me. When time came for me to resume the jazz, she invited me to join her and the others at her hotel which was the Hotel Norwich, after I had finished.

At 10pm when we handed over to the next band, I felt very tired, too tired to travel across Norwich to keep the rendez-vous. Two weeks later, on my return to Boswell's, Brian handed me a letter marked: 'To the Piano Player, Boswell's Pub, Norwich, England'.

It was, of course, a letter from Kathleen Bracken who expressed her disappointment at not seeing me on that evening at her hotel and asked if I would write to her. I did so and she and I corresponded for a long time with fairly long detailed letters through which a strong friendship grew. Such was the strength of that friendship, that birthday and Christmas presents were exchanged, even from her to my daughter.

When, in 1994, I announced my engagement and forthcoming marriage to Miriam, Kathleen from her home in Richmond, Virginia, sent us a beautiful wedding gift of a 'William and Mary' trivet.

In 1998 we made the trip to Virginia, where we spent two memorable weeks, Kathleen and her family and friends overwhelming us with their generosity and hospitality. During our stay we were taken to the Blue Ridge Mountains and the beautiful city of Washington with our hostess and her family paying for almost everything, including hotel bills.

All this, you might say, because of a chance meeting at a jazz gig.

'A Pretty Girl is Like a Melody' wrote Irving Berlin, little realizing how the song would be synonymous with mannequin parades for many years. I used it, together with others like 'Lovely Lady' and 'Sweet and Lovely' for two such parades, one at Breckland Hall, Costessey and the other at Central Hall, Wymondham. The one at Costessey was a straightforward display of ladies' fashions while the Wymondham venue included some children's and party dresses, two gigs which added yet another dimension to my musical experience.

At Brasteds' restaurant, at Framingham Pigot, where a big charity dinner was held, I was asked to play in two places, though not at the same time. The first was in a large foyer or vestibule on Brasteds' own upright which I think may have been a Monington and Weston, one of the better English makes. Aperitifs, canapés and the like were being served there to my background music but as the numbers of black tied gentlemen and their ladies grew, so did the volume of conversation, drowning me completely. In fact it was so loud I couldn't hear a single thing I was playing, when a gentleman tapped me on the shoulder.

"I know," I yelled above the din, "I played a bum note."

"No, no, it's not that," he shouted, "I just love the way you play Gershwin."

Clearly a man of taste and apparently very acute hearing.

Part two of the evening was held in a large marquee where I had already set up my keyboard to play through supper until I was substituted by John MacGregor in his rôle as magician.

Any disasters as solo player ? Well, just one outstanding evening comes easily to mind when I was booked by Benny Lyon for a gig in Lowestoft.

"Hotel, private party, background music," he said, never being a man of many words, but in fact all three parts of his instruction could not have been more wrong.

The 'hotel' in a none too salubrious quarter of the town, turned out to be a large pub. There was no 'private party' but I had to set up in a bar where a number of characters were already gathered, giving the appearance of those who had passed auditions for parts in a production of *On the Waterfront*, one of them being a dead ringer for Lee J Cobb. 'Background Music' it was not but I was expected to be the pub entertainer for the night and me with no Equity card either.

A singer, who obviously performed there regularly, asked me if I could accompany him to some Sinatra to which I said yes, and to some Neil Diamond to which I said no, having seen the dots.

After a spell of my playing, the landlord came and asked the question I had been expecting and one which a thousand pianists abhor: "Can't you play something lively?"

Ken Meazey, a fine pianist friend, told me he was playing at an army dinner when one young low-ranking officer, slightly the worse for drink, came and asked Ken that very question.

"I play dinner music," said Ken. "If you want lively music there's a disco in the next room." Most succinct, a good answer.

I made feeble attempts to 'liven up' my performance but very soon mine host came to me and not unkindly indicated to me that it was not what they wanted at which point I felt I should explain to him the basis on which I had been booked. He was very understanding, agreeing to settle with some 'petrol money' and I packed my gear away, much to the dismay of half a dozen elderly customers who declared that my music had been 'the best thing they had heard in weeks'.

In 1992, I went on one of Mike Sutcliffe's Leisureline Holidays, during the course of which I and the other travellers found ourselves in Venice, in St Mark's Square.

There were hundreds of tourists, thousands of pigeons and three small orchestras situated under canopies at the side of the square. We all went to listen to one of them, a trio of piano (a grand), double bass and violin, although the pianist leader had clearly given up his stool to a tourist 'guest', albeit on a temporary basis. The 'guest', an Italian I believe, had taken command of the grand piano for some time which was why the leader, when asked by the English party if their friend (me) could play, said with tight-lipped stance:

"Uno."

I took my place at the black grand and witnessing that there were a great many Americans round me opted to play 'Misty' by Errol Garner, in E flat as written. Within seconds, the bass player joined me, quickly followed by the girl on the violin and in the second chorus, the leader, seating himself next to me, added some extemporary bits at the top end of the piano.

Everybody clapped with cries of "encore" but the leader was having none of it, repeating his earlier threat with some emphasis:

"Non! Uno."

I heeded him and not the onlookers, many of whom were clearly fans of Mr Garner. I left the rostrum and rightly so: an encore would have been highly unprofessional, something which I have seen happen all too often. Nevertheless it was a moment to treasure and I began to reflect on the fact that since I had now played in Canada and Italy, could I put on a business card 'International Pianist'?

My Alter Ego cut in straight away: "Certainly not – far too pretentious."

My most memorable moment as a solo pianist came, following a private engagement, at Norwich's Hotel Nelson.

Several of the diners and I had noticed a couple come into the adjacent public restaurant, recognizing them as Mr and Mrs Bill Pertwee, he the warden in TV's *Dad's Army*. The diners persuaded me to play 'Who Do You Think You Are Kidding Mister Hitler?', the programme's signature tune composed by Jimmy Perry and David Croft.

At the end of the evening, as I was packing up, Bill Pertwee and his wife came through.

"I hope you didn't mind my playing that song," I said.

"Mind? Do you know, a man could never have had twenty-five happier years than I spent with them. Twenty-five wonderful years."

I thought: "What an epitaph for all those remarkable men."

When Miriam and I took friends, David and Rosemary Williams, to Holkham Hall in North Norfolk, we discovered a lovely black grand in the vast hall entrance way, standing just by the foot of the marble staircase. The note on the piano read: 'This piano is meant to be played. Any competent pianist is welcome to do so'.

The signature was that of Lady Coke.

I could not resist such a chance and sat down to play a Gershwin selection into which I became completely absorbed. When I had finished there came loud applause from quite a crowd of visitors standing in the hall or on the stairs. Most rewarding.

Up to now in this chapter I have spoken mainly about me as the chap on a 'tinkling piano', but what of all the others who have graced the many keyboards of Norfolk? Of course, pianists or piano players rarely meet, there being no piano players' conventions or meetings of the Black and White Club. More's the pity I think.

Note that I used the term piano player: my late friend, Scotsman Jimmy Skene, had to be very careful with the word 'pianist', misheard or misconstrued on several occasions which was the reason he referred to them as piano players.

Sadly, some of them have passed on, such as the highly-gifted Ken Hewitt who played piano for a long time at the Savoy Hotel in Norwich with The

Dick Kenden Sound. Likewise there was the eccentric, but brilliant, Stan Jennings of whom many tales are told, such as when he had holes in the knees of his dress trousers, blacked in his knee caps with black felt tip pen.

David Denny was a Scot who could read anything but busk nothing and long after he had ended his playing career would come to The Oaklands for Sunday lunch, when he would send me request notes. His favourite song was 'But Beautiful", a song Bing Crosby sang in one of his *Road* films.

The man of a thousand tunes was the late Jack Andrews who would play two dozen numbers for say, a quickstep without stopping, an acknowledged eccentric. I visited him in his retirement home in Goldsmith Street where we chatted for hours and since he had no piano I took him a dummy keyboard. He couldn't have been more delighted. He told me he had a very good friend who owned a hotel in Leicester and that quite regularly, this friend would make the journey from Leicester to Norwich, take Jack back with him to play the piano in his hotel, in return for which, having full board and paying Jack a fee. After the weekend his friend would bring Jack all the way back to Norwich.

It sounded almost unbelievable and I think Jack himself could hardly believe his luck. Certainly his piano playing must have been worth it, not only to the hotelier but also his guests.

Among my contemporaries is Dennis Payne, formerly bass player in my Rémon Quartet, who has found solo keyboard work so useful, being a long-time regular at The Petersfield Hotel at Horning. When he and his wife Barbara went on a cruise on a Greek ship, Dennis was impressed with the dance band and, in particular, a certain tune they played one evening while he and Barbara were dancing. He asked the leader if they could play it again and was astounded at the reply:

"We play it again, tomorrow night at twenty past nine."

Modern pre-programmed medleys had clearly reached the Greek musicians.

Dennis also astounded me when he told me of his conversation with a pianist from a trio on one cruise he and Barbara had. They had enjoyed the music greatly and Dennis complimented the pianist, who at once knew that Dennis was from England.

"What part of England are you from?" he asked and Dennis said he was from Norfolk.

"I did some gigs in Norwich," said the pianist, "at Samson's Hall."

"You mean The Samson and Hercules," corrected Dennis.

"Yes, that's right. I played piano there for Jan Ralfini."

Dennis then told the pianist that he had played with the second string band at the time, namely The Rémon Quartet and that when the band came to change over with the other they would play 'Tenderly', a waltz in E flat. I'm not sure who was the more amazed: the cruise pianist or Dennis. What a small world it is.

Pianists of the past include Billy Duncan, legendary big band leader in Norwich and Derek Warne, one time accompanist to Anna at Norwich's Jolly Butchers and who went on to become Ted Heath's pianist and arranger. Others I hold in high esteem are Roger Cooke, Derek Standley and Arthur Maton, all of whom have depped for me over the years and Steve Battle, keyboard and organist extraordinary. Then there is Barry Bryant who has worked with me in shows, as well as sharing the duties of a 'silent cinema' pianist. Barry, in his 'fifties obtained a music degree at the University of East Anglia – most commendable.

Mike Cochrane, a much-travelled man took over my duties as Keep Fit pianist for Betty Phillp at Cringleford, while two other keyboard friends in the big band world are Ken Meazey, already mentioned in this chapter, and Peter Fenn, former musical director at Anglia Television. Peter, a superb master of the piano, now retired from TV, jokes about the many times he has been asked:

"Did you used to be Peter Fenn?"

It is Peter who graciously agreed to write the foreword to this book.

Good accompanists are a rare breed but they do exist in our part of the world. David Kett has accompanied shows, groups, singers and concert parties so well for as long as I can remember, while excellent rehearsal men are Ian Shepherd, Christian Stirling and Adrian Turner.

The ladies, too, play their part: the splendid Jackie Brightman and Annette Jude, the latter playing for 'Wings of Song' Ladies Choir and who is a dear friend. The quiet and dependable Mary Bettany has been the stalwart pianist for the Judy Habbitts' dancing school for more years than she can care to remember.

Among those on the fringe of my music circle is the highly versatile Mike Capocci who during his intricate extemporizations manages to 'quote' from a great many other numbers. I've listened to him many times, never failing to be impressed by his dexterity in the jazz style, reminiscent of Bill Evans, someone I know Mike admires greatly.

Still on that same fringe are the classical pianists all of whom I greatly respect with names like Peter Wills, whom I knew well in my teaching days, Vaughan Brooks, Bob Yates' regular accompanist, Peter Cooper, so accomplished and Rita Berchem, formerly pianist for 'Wings of Song', all wonderful readers.

Anyone who plays the piano has a list of performers at pro level that they idolize and in this respect I am no different. Some, because they hail from a former age, I never saw, only able to listen to them on record: pianists like Billy Mayerl, composer of many 'flower' tunes, mostly quite fiendish to play; Carroll Gibbons, the slow-spoken American with the beautiful touch; Leslie Hutchinson ('Hutch') who played at the top hotels, becoming an icon of high society; Charlie Kunz, another American whose style was unique to the point that you knew at once it was he playing.

Still in this country I loved Steve Race's skill, the delightful presentation of Albert Semprini – 'Old ones, new ones, forgotten ones, neglected ones', Ronnie Price on *Name That Tune* and Stanley Black, a master at the keyboard and composer to boot.

From the States came more great names like Oscar Levant, the po-faced pianist who figured in the story of George Gershwin, Eddie Duchin, who died so young from leukaemia, Nat 'King' Cole, a fine jazz artist before he became a world-renowned vocalist and Peter Nero, he with the incredible lightning fingers. Whatever one may say about Liberace, he was a superb pianist as well as a showman, his entire act being so very professional. And speaking of performers, I enjoy listening to Michael Feinstein when he presents his illustrated programmes about legendary composers. I'm not sure of Carman Cavallero's birthplace, but his piano playing rates highly on my list, and it was he who played the sound track in *The Eddie Duchin Story*.

Roy Budd was a pianist I loved to hear, a man who composed film music and also led a very talented trio, rather like the blind George Shearing who delighted so many with his 'close chord' work. I saw him twice at Norwich Theatre Royal, both magical evenings for me.

So did I ever meet any of the pros? Yes, two.

Before he was due to go on at a seaside show, I went to meet Joe ('Mr Piano') Henderson, a most delightful and modest man.

"I just play all the old songs in the only way I know how and people seem to love it," he said.

What more can you do than that? I do remember his catchy little signature tune, his own composition called 'Trudie', a great favourite of the tap classes.

The other man I met I mentioned in my first book *S'Wonderful*: he was Dick Katz, pianist to the Ray Ellington Quartet, a master on the ivories and a perfect gentleman. We met twice: the first time at Banham Pavilion, where he autographed my sheet music and the second at Norwich's Samson and Hercules.

"A tinkling piano in the next apartment...." runs the lyric.

I wonder where my next apartment will be?

CHAPTER SIXTEEN

Thank You
For The Music

THIS final chapter brings my life story up to date and, like the two-headed god Janus, will look back at the past, forward to the future with a bit in the middle being a glance at the present.

In almost six and a half decades I have seen so much change in the world of music with my story tracing its way through from the last of the Golden Years to the Second World War with its tragic but beautiful songs, through the tuneful 'Fifties, marred only by the advent of 'Rock and Roll', which the knowledgeable Anna of The Jolly Butchers affirmed originated from the movement of coitus, and then into the radical 'Sixties, a decade which for me holds no charm. In the remaining years I have enjoyed the friendship of some fine musicians and have tried to keep my head, 'when (seemingly) all about are losing theirs'.

In those six and a half decades I have accomplished much and have learned much, for musicians never stop learning since music knows no boundaries. There have been so many wonderful people along my journey that have helped and influenced me, not least of all my parents, who first sowed the seeds from which my music would grow, and Nina Warmoll, the lady who breathed into me the inspiration, the magic that made it start to happen.

Encouragement came from many sources: my first wife Jane, who helped me so much in my work as a school's head of music. My Aunt Edith, who through my childhood to youth gave me such help and advice and all those in my family who may have fancied that here was a budding Mozart or even a Gershwin!

Music brought me so many great friends, most of whom I have written about in both books, such as the members of my superb Rémon Quartet, including those who sang with us, the incredible Jimmy Skene – Norfolk's own Stephane Grappelli – and those who made up 'Tony and Friends', not least of all my wife Miriam.

Others were Don Hoffmann, who used to delight so many old folk with his powerful singing, Paul Donley of Yare Valley Jazz and Edward Murray-Harvey, he of the barrel organs and massive sheet music library.

Those in the world of music I have held (and still hold) in great admiration are Yehudi Menhuin, Steve Race, George Mitchell, George Gershwin and the former director for music for Norfolk schools, Fred Firth. And that bit in the middle – the present?

Well, I continue to provide 'wallpaper music', a programme of songs and music for old folk and also music for the 'silent cinema'.

After a recent perfomance at Cinema City, a couple came up to me and asked: "How do you do it all? How can you keep it up for the entire film with no music?" I just do and it comes from an accumulation of musical knowledge, learning and experience. At hotel venues someone will say: "I wish I could play like you." or "I wish I'd kept up my playing."

Of course, it didn't just happen: such things don't generally – they come with practice and a lot of hard work. In 'Sparky's Magic Piano', a record often requested way back in Children's Favourites, it was the piano that played incredibly difficult pieces, not Sparky. Yet his mother thought he had somehow acquired a tremendous talent, a gift for playing. Rarely does that happen, as we all know. The majority of us have to work up to it.

My dear late friend Hazel Fletcher was teaching in school where the head said that every class had to perform a song at the concert and each teacher would be its accompanist at the piano. Now Hazel knew nothing about piano playing but always loyal to the cause, she had the head of school music write out a very simple accompaniment on a sheet of manuscript paper for her. Hazel practised hard; my, how she practised until she had it right. Came the concert, Hazel sitting at the piano when her class's turn came with the head announcing: "And now it is the turn of Miss Fletcher's class…"

Hazel raised her hands ready poised to play when a sudden gust of wind blew her music sheet gently from the piano across the floor. Thus she never played; all that practice wasted, all for nothing. Fortunately, Hazel's sense of humour prevailed which was clearly evident when she told the tale against herself.

Recording comes within my musical frame these days, since I can tape directly from my Roland or my Technics with a Dolby unit which is handy inasmuch that any extraneous sounds do not appear and the door-bell, a cough or a passing car are not included. I have taped tap routines for eighty-year-olds and background music for widows and widowers, all of whom seem highly pleased, coming back for more. My 'commercial" tapes – *Candlelight Piano* and *Recalling the 'Fifties* didn't exactly jump to the top ten in W H Smith's, but people who bought them seemed to enjoy what they heard, reminders of yesteryear and a realization that there isn't a great deal of musicality on offer today. We have a noise-ridden society with a multitude of groups calling themselves 'bands' pounding out more noise at a volume that music colleague Peter Fenn describes as 'pain level'. Some of the females of that breed can be heard in many a store on records which reminds my wife of a hospital labour ward. There are endless 'charts' showing these stars' placings, no doubt according to how many discs they sell, and I find it difficult at times to know which is the song and which is the name of the group.

Of course, all this presents a generation gap which has become as wide as the Grand Canyon for which much of the blame must lie with the media, in particular television and radio. When did you last see a British music programme on television? When a show? When variety with some musical content? Lesley Garrett had a four week run and that was it.

I watched the New Year's Day concert from Vienna, a superb musical presentation and to cap that a programme of orchestral, band and vocal music given by a charismatic Dutchman called Andre Rieu, who is stunning European audiences with his talented young musicians and singers. Why aren't we producing such things? Write to the television authorities who reply that such shows are not 'visually stimulating', something to which I do not deign to comment.

So how can I be positive about music programmes returning to the television, which after all, has to be the mightiest medium in the world. The TV merchants were able to give us *What the Victorians did for us* and *The History of Britain*, so why not a series tracing the story of popular music and song?

They made a half-baked attempt with the story of jazz, which tended to concentrate too much on racism and not nearly enough on the music, but such a suggestion as I have made would be an ideal way to show younger people how popular music evolved. Maybe 'not stimulating enough'.

Radio Two makes small attempts with biopics of various composers like Richard Rodgers in his centenary year but such programmes are on so late at night with the rest of each week day almost a carbon copy of Radio One. Sunday is the only real 'music day'.

In my youth, during the summer months, the BBC, aware that people's windows would be open, appealed to radio listeners to keep their volume down in consideration for others. It is an indication of how public self-discipline has changed vastly since those days, when our ears and our very minds are assailed by hellish monkey music from houses, cafes and other buildings, as well as open-windowed cars. There was no such thing as 'musak', and the relayed type of music I remember would be at fairgrounds with the familiar organ, at football matches with stirring marches of Sousa or Kenneth Alford or in the cinema before the film or in the interval. Occasionally, a theatre organist would appear out of the depths to play a selection of music, from popular songs to current shows and I never failed to marvel at his dexterity with hands and feet coping with so many stops and sounds.

Vainly I look for a modern day pianist of any note (no pun) and recently did spot the splendid Laurie Holloway, albeit in the shadows, backing the *Michael Parkinson Show* but there's precious little, which means resorting to tapes and CDs to hear the masters.

My daughter Elisabeth, who has kept the music going, particularly in the world of the stage, singing and dancing in shows like *Hello Dolly, Mack and Mabel* and *My Fair Lady*, presented me with a framed poem entitled: "Poems on the Underground" by D H Lawrence. It is something I like to read regularly as it hangs in my study:

> *"Softly, in the dusk, a woman is singing to me;*
> *Taking me back down the vista of years, till I see*
> *A child sitting under the piano in the boom of the tingling strings*
> *And pressing the small poised feet of a mother who smiles as she sings.*
> *In spite of myself, the insidious mastery of song*
> *Betrays me back, till the heart of me weeps to belong*
> *To the old Sunday evenings at home, with winter outside,*
> *And hymns in the cosy parlour, the tinkling piano our guide.*
> *So now it is vain for the singer to burst into clamour*
> *With the great black piano appassionato. The glamour*
> *Of childish days is upon me, my manhood is cast*
> *Down in the flood of remembrance, I weep like a child for the past."*

I hear what Lawrence says but realise you can't bring back the past, many aspects of which are best left there, but some of the past, such as its music, is a heritage that should be preserved so that generations to come may, at the very least, be aware of it.

Do you have a favourite song? This question is directed at me so often, the simple answer being no, but since most songs concern themselves with love, I have two which relate to the two lovely ladies who have been Mrs Ireland in my life.

For my late Jane, Charles Stroud's song 'Once Upon a Time' has the nostalgic and wistful lines:

> *"Once upon a time, a girl with sunlight in her hair*
> *Put her hand in mine*
> *And said she loved me*
> *But that was once upon a time*
> *Very long ago."*